HOSTILITY

HOSTILITY

LESTER SUMRALL

Thomas Nelson Publishers
Nashville

Copyright © 1981 by Lester Sumrall Evangelistic Association, Inc.

Published in Nashville, Tennessee, by Thomas Nelson, Inc., Publishers and distributed in Canada by Lawson Falle, Ltd., Cambridge, Ontario.

ISBN 0-8407-5765-4

Contents

1. Hostility: Who, What, Where? 9
2. What Causes Hostility? 16
3. The Effects of Hostility 38
4. The Mind and Hostility 48
5. Hostility Towards God and God's Children . . . 58
6. Do-It-Yourself Kits 67
7. What Jesus Said and Did About Hostility . . . 76
8. Hostility and the End Times 89
9. Facing Up to Hostility 102
10. How to Destroy Hostility 108

HOSTILITY

Chapter 1

HOSTILITY: WHO, WHAT, WHERE?

"THREE KILLED, FOUR INJURED IN SENSELESS
  MURDER SPREE"

"WAR THREATENS MIDDLE EAST"

"VANDALS DESTROY ELEMENTARY SCHOOL
  CLASSROOM"

"HOSPITAL SUED FOR MALPRACTICE"

Sound familiar? Just pick up a newspaper any day,
any place in the world, and you will read similar head-
lines. Never before have so many angry, hurting,
hostile people openly vented their rage against other
individuals, businesses, countries, and society at
large. Hostility touches everyone, regardless of race
or nationality. It is a universal problem of epidemic
proportions.

Hostility Defined

The word "hostile" comes from the Latin *hostilis,* meaning "enemy." One dictionary defines it as "an unfriendly attitude; antagonism, opposition, or resistance in thought or principle." In reality, it is a deadly venom capable of robbing us of joy, peace, healthy relationships, and life itself.

Hostility is an emotional problem that can best be dealt with by the application of spiritual truths. Because it cripples human personalities and dwarfs the spirit and mind if not cleansed by confession and forgiveness, it soon spreads to contaminate all other emotions. What starts as a tiny germ of bitterness or anger can erupt into emotional instability and manifest itself in a variety of physical illnesses. Worst of all, it is highly contagious; a hostile person can cause others to become abrasive. This negative emotion passes from friend to friend, parent to child, teacher to student, and from governments to whole nations.

Hostility is one of Satan's most effective weapons, separating man from man and man from God. And no one is immune—not you, not me.

Two Sides of Anger

As beings created in the image of God, we have been instilled with a full spectrum of human emotions. Emotions can be either positive or negative. Too often, however, they are labeled as acceptable or unacceptable without understanding what triggered the feelings in the first place. Our capacity to experience emotions is one of God's most precious gifts; this was demonstrated in Christ's own personality. Anger is the emotion most often associated with hostility, yet anger is not always sinful.

The Bible shows us that God Himself, who is the essence of love, is fully capable of anger. In the Old Testament alone the word "anger" appears over 450 times, and 375 of those references relate to God's anger.

According to author David Augsburger:

> Conflict is neither good nor bad, right or wrong. Conflict simply is. How we view, approach and work through our differences does—to a large extent—determine our whole life pattern.[1]

Ephesians 4:26 says, "Be ye angry, and sin not. . . ." God understands the necessity of expressing, rather than repressing, feelings such as anger. It is partly the purpose of this book to help Christians deal with potentially destructive emotions in a biblical manner, for it is out of the festering brew of unconfessed and unresolved hatred, anger, fear, and resentment that hostility is born.

Let us then carefully define hostility *not* as the flash of emotion that comes in response to a painful or unpleasant situation, but rather as the result of harboring those feelings in an unforgiving attitude of resentment.

The last half of Ephesians 4:26 says, ". . . let not the sun go down upon your wrath." This implies that one should resolve his differences with others and deal with his feelings of anger as soon as possible. Hostility becomes a problem when we allow our angry feelings to fester. Just as an infected wound left unattended can result in the development of gangrene, so unresolved hostility can become destructive and hinder our relations with others and with God Himself.

There is no virtue in clinging stubbornly to one's "rights." Hebrews 12:14 advises that we "Follow peace with all men, and holiness, without which no man shall see the Lord," and verse 15 explains why, cautioning, ". . . lest any root of bitterness springing up trouble you, and thereby many be defiled."

Jesus spoke of the folly of being unwilling to give up one's hostile feelings. "For if ye forgive men their trespasses, your heavenly Father will also forgive you: But if ye forgive not men their trespasses, neither will your Father forgive your trespasses" (Matt. 6:14,15). Plainly, the consequences of hanging onto hostility are too great—we risk blocking God's forgiveness.

Where Are All the Hostile Humans?

In the deepest jungles of Africa, we see animals preying upon one another in order to survive. Yet hostility by our definition is not often found in the animal kingdom; rarely do we see an animal kill out of greed or for revenge. Only when he is hungry, wounded, frightened, or agitated does he become a hostile killer.

Unfortunately, this is not always true of people. Not only do we display hostility when we feel threatened by something or someone outside ourselves, but we are fully capable of being moved to hostility by greed, hate, or revenge.

In more primitive areas of the world there exist whole tribes of hostile people whose culture is steeped in hatred, deceit, and distrust of anyone outside their understanding, and when it doesn't get it, it often violence is considered a desirable trait and actually is encouraged.

But we cannot pretend that this kind of hostility is confined to the more isolated areas of the globe. Many people today live in emotional jungles of despair, discontent, and disappointment. Hostility is a living volcano of resentment erupting in our homes, our schools, and our cities. It infects the educated as well as the uneducated; the rich as well as the poor. The young. The old. Believers and nonbelievers alike. It seeps its way into the hearts and minds of its most zealous opponents, turning the very body of Christ against itself. We cannot continue to hold this problem at arm's length, refusing to claim it as our own. Hostility is not just our neighbors' problem; it can be found in our own homes. It doesn't exist only in our enemies' hearts, but in our own also.

Human history is a study of hostility. Wars, revolutions, murders, deceit—rarely has the course of human events been altered drastically by anything but hostile means. The Bible is full of examples: Cain's hostility towards Abel; Esau's hostility towards Isaac; King Saul's towards David; the Pharisees' towards Jesus—all examples of hostility that changed the course of history.

Today our cities seethe with hostility. The Watts riots of the sixties and the 1980 racial violence in Florida stand out as tragic examples of the tremendous force of destruction released when the "volcano" finally erupts. But such demonstrations are only symptomatic of the inner rage and hostility of men and women we pass on the street, or go to school with, or work with each day. Dr. Karl A. Menninger attributes the growing violence to the population explosion and crowded living conditions. He says that crowding people together aggravates tensions and causes irritations that make us more prone to violence.

Recently I was in New York City; a few blocks from my hotel I stopped a policeman to ask the quickest way back.

He looked at me sternly and said, "Sir, I am a policeman with a gun, and if I were going to your hotel I'd take a cab."

I blinked my eyes a couple of times and said, "I am out for a walk."

"No," he said, "you're out to die. This is New York."

I took a cab.

Of course, all of us are aware of the dangers of walking in certain areas of our larger cities, but even the streets of small towns and the nicer residential areas are becoming unsafe. Our society has learned to live behind locked doors and barred windows. We glance nervously over our shoulders at the sound of hurried footsteps coming up behind us, even in broad daylight on a busy street; and we warn our children not to talk to strangers.

Our world is literally destroying itself through hostility. The very earth seems to be rebelling against the rape of its natural resources and the pollution of its air and water. We live in constant fear of nuclear war or economic disaster.

As Christians we view the growing hostility in the world from another perspective. Luke 21:9–28 warns of wars, commotions, nation fighting against nation, and the persecution and imprisonment of Christians. It speaks of Christian parents, brethren, kinsfolk, and friends being betrayed and even put to death. Hatred will abound; these will be days of vengeance and distress among nations. Having been warned of all this, we are told "when these things begin to come to pass, then look up, and lift up your heads; for your redemption draweth nigh" (Luke 21:28).

There is a message for humanity in this hostile age. "Wake up! Recognize where we are. The King is coming and the end of this world is near!"

Christians have a tremendous responsibility during these last days. We will soon witness the greatest explosion of naked, brutal hostility in the history of mankind.

Chapter 2

WHAT CAUSES HOSTILITY?

Hostility is a spiritual affliction of the mind and heart. It is not inborn, as some would have us believe. Aggressionist Konrad Lorenz declares:

> Aggression, in the proper and narrower sense of the word, is the fighting instinct in beast and man which is directed against members of the same species. It serves that species by balancing the distribution of its members over the available environment and by selecting the most rugged members to do the reproducing of the species.[1]

This view labels human beings as simply a more highly developed form of animal life, evolved from the ape and at the mercy of their baser instincts.

This is in direct contradiction to the biblical revelation that man was created uniquely in the image of God and was given dominion over the rest of creation. Certainly such a creature has the ability to control his own emotions and actions.

Hostility is not caused by a person's "hot Irish blood" or "fiery Latin temper." Cultural background cannot be blamed for an individual's lack of emotional discipline. No one is born hostile. Rather, children are born with a natural ability to vent their emotions in a healthy way, preventing the buildup of anger and frustration that leads to hostility. That is why one moment they can be crying as if their hearts would break, and the next moment they are playing happily without a care in the world. They deal with each feeling as it comes.

Hostility's Roots

The roots of hostility cannot legitimately be traced to past hurts or disappointments. In his book *Man and Aggression,* Ashley Montagu claims that the kind of behavior a person displays in any circumstance is determined largely by his past experiences. For unregenerate people, locked within the prison of their past sin and failure, this may be true. But when Jesus died on the cross and rose again, He broke our bondage to the past and freed every believer to make right choices in every area of our lives. Whether we do so or not is our own responsibility.

Sin, not nature, is the cause of hostility. It came first out of the pride of the angel Lucifer, who sought to exalt himself above God. Ezekiel 28:17 speaks of his pride and its consequences.

Thine heart was lifted up because of thy beauty, thou hast corrupted thy wisdom by reason of thy brightness: I will cast thee to the ground, I will lay thee before kings, that they may behold thee.

Hostility's Backbone

Pride is the backbone of hostility. Pride keeps us rigid—unwilling to bend until we see the other person broken, unwilling to forgive unless the other person confesses and seeks forgiveness, unwilling to forget until the situation is resolved and *we* have been justified. Pride can keep us from reaching out a conciliatory hand when we are wrong, and especially when we are right. More marriages fall victim to this kind of unwillingness to give than to any other social or emotional problem.

A young pastor once shared with a group of husbands a discipline the Lord was working in his life. "No matter how wrong I think my wife is or how right I think I am, I know that after the storm is over I am to make the first move towards smoothing the troubled waters between us. I am the head of my household and must love my wife as Jesus loved the church. To me that means dying to self enough to be the first one to say, 'I'm sorry.' By that, I am not always saying, 'I've changed my mind. You're right and I'm wrong,' but I am saying, 'I love you and I appreciate your feelings and am willing to talk things through.' "

Pride gives place to a myriad of other sins, such as selfish ambition, which was Lucifer's downfall.

How art thou fallen from heaven, O Lucifer, son of the morning! how art thou cut down to the ground, which didst weaken the nations! For thou hast said in thine heart, I will ascend into heaven, I will exalt my throne above the stars of God: I will sit also upon the mount of the congregation, in the sides of the north: I will ascend above the heights of the clouds; I will be like the most High (Is. 14:12–14).

Through Satan, sin and hostility were transmitted to a sinless earth and passed to Adam and Eve in the form of rebellion against God. Again, the selfish ambition to "be as gods, knowing good and evil" was the enticement (Gen. 3:5). Once sin entered the human race, it was passed from generation to generation, and hostility was born.

And the LORD God said unto the serpent, Because thou hast done this . . . I will put enmity between thee and the woman, and between thy seed and her seed; it shall bruise thy head, and thou shalt bruise his heel (Gen. 3:14,15).

This hostility was to be between Eve's seed and Satan, not between men. Satan takes this natural enmity very seriously. He despises mankind and does everything in his power to keep us from discovering the reality of life in Jesus Christ. Failing that, he taunts, confuses, tempts, and accuses, attacking any way he can to prevent believers from fully understanding and effectively using the spiritual weapons and authority that are theirs according to the Word of God and before which Satan cannot stand.

Is it any wonder that hostility runs rampant across the face of the earth?

Any number of negative feelings can lead to hostility. The everyday tensions, pressures, and frustrations of living in our fast-paced society provide a hothouse environment for emotional hostilities. Anxiety levels have never been higher. Spiraling inflation, changing moral and social standards, and the general lack of optimism in the world today have provided people with a whole new set of worries and fears. They feel themselves losing control of their lives. Without the security of a personal relationship with the One who holds the future in His hand, people often feel they are at the mercy of their circumstances. This unsettling state of affairs sets them on edge, ready to release their tension over the smallest offense.

Prayer Power

God has a different suggestion—prayer.

Be careful for nothing; but in every thing by prayer and supplication with thanksgiving let your requests be made known unto God. And the peace of God, which passeth all understanding, shall keep your hearts and minds through Christ Jesus (Phil. 4:6,7).

A young man who was struggling with his Christian walk asked his grandfather, a dear saint of God, just how he managed not only to stay strong in his faith for over eighty years, but how he did so with such obvious joy and peace.

"I've never seen you angry or irritable or even discouraged. What's your secret?" the grandson asked.

"It's simple," replied the old man, with a smile.

"Each morning I wake up early and get on my knees in prayer. And I don't get up until I feel His wonderful joy and peace flood my heart. Then I know I am ready to face whatever the day may bring."

Few of us have that kind of unruffled demeanor. And few of us see that kind of an even-keeled disposition in those around us. Why not? Without doubt it relates to the time we invest in equipping ourselves to face the enemy's onslaughts.

Prayer is a key. Power to stand up to whatever the day may bring can come as we saturate our minds with the joy of the Lord. As we spend time in unbroken communion with Him—through prayer and reading the Bible—we will find ourselves better able to face whatever comes our way. It may sound simplistic, but it is a proven method of doing combat with our adversary, the devil.

Competition

Competitiveness—in business, on a social level, in school, sports, and politics—can result in deep-seated hostility if it is not carefully identified and dealt with. We in the United States have been brought up to believe that the best man always wins; so if we don't win or at least make a showing close to the top, we take it as a commentary on our worth. This stirs up feelings of insecurity and inferiority, two more key roots of hostility.

It has been observed that to a great degree the amount of hostility produced in an individual is directly related to his feelings of inferiority at the time. It is much easier to be kind, sympathetic, and unselfish after accomplishment than after failure.

Not everyone achieves in ways that are recognized by society. Sometimes accomplishment seems to evade all but extremely gifted individuals. But the failure to recognize real accomplishment lies in our definition of what achievement is. We are too narrow in our thinking. A mother may be as accomplished in her role of soothing a troubled child as her husband is in negotiating a big contract for the company that employs him. But too often the mother feels frustrated and inferior and comes to the end of a busy day with hostile feelings, ready to explode.

The consequences of excessive feelings of inferiority are graphically illustrated in the rise and fall of Adolph Hitler. It was because of the crushing defeat and humiliating reparations of World War I that the German people were so susceptible to a leader who stood for superiority and hatred.

Our Hostile Children

Parents can be a prime source of hostility in their children. A lack of trust and affirmation in the home can produce a growing snowball of anger and frustration within a child. If this is not melted by the warmth of honest communication and expressions of love, it can freeze parents and child into positions of constant confrontation.

Recently a well-known television performer talked about his relationship with his pastor-father. He talked with great admiration about his father's powerful pulpit ministry. His father's preaching exuded the love of God, and many souls were saved.

"Then," the man went on, "he would step down from the pulpit, take me by the hand, and we would go home. Just like that, my father would change from the living expression of love and concern he was to the congregation, to an aloof, undemonstrative man who never once put his arms around me or told me he loved me."

My heart went out to that young man as the camera closed in on his tortured expression. "I never have been able to understand how God could love me when my father didn't," he confessed.

Sibling rivalry is another painful result of parents not being sensitive to their children's needs and feelings. There is nothing more painful for a child than the feeling that he is less loved and appreciated than his brother or sister.

The story of Joseph and his brothers is a classic illustration of this problem. Angry and hurt that their father loved Joseph more than he loved them and openly favored him, his brothers sold Joseph into slavery, telling their father that he had been killed.

Many children are constantly trying to live up to the accomplishments of older brothers and sisters. Some feel pushed aside emotionally when a new baby comes into the family. Their pain and hostility may be equal to or even greater than Joseph's brothers' and will probably leave scars that they will carry into their adult lives and relationships.

The outside world is going to do enough emotional damage to children who aren't quite as bright, talented, or attractive as their siblings; the home should be a place where their self-worth is reinforced, where they know they are loved and accepted just as they are.

The unending pressure of meeting a child's physical and emotional needs can produce another form of hostility. Most parents battle this in silence, ashamed that they are capable of feeling such strong negative emotions toward their own children. I could read the distress and guilt on one young mother's face as she sat in my office and described her experience.

Nancy was an attractive, intelligent, basically happy mother of three small children, ages one, three, and five. She and Bill wanted to have their children two years apart, as they felt it would be nice for the children to play together and that it would give the family a sense of unity.

Normally Nancy copes with the constant demands of her offspring with good humor and loving patience, but one day was an exception. The house, which was usually kept in reasonable order, reflected her mood. Beds were unmade, dishes were stacked in the sink, and toys were scattered from one end of the house to the other.

Nancy viewed the scene with fatalistic pessimism. The idea of making one bed or washing one dish overwhelmed her. Her body felt drained of all energy, and her nerves were raw and sensitive. From the moment she woke up she knew it was going to be "one of those days," and she was right.

The children immediately picked up on Nancy's depression and (as small children seem to do) responded by becoming whiney and even more demanding than usual. The house was filled with the sound of their shrill little screams and shouts of "Mommy, Billy pulled my hair" or "Mommy, I had the toy first and Susie won't give it back."

Irritating as the constant noise was, it was the quiet lulls in between that demanded immediate investigation. Children are rarely quiet unless they have found something fascinating to do, like trying on Mommy's makeup or sampling the pretty "candy" in the medicine cabinet.

Nancy found herself walking an emotional tightrope. Her irritation grew with each additional crisis and demand, threatening to push her off balance. The intensity of her emotions was frightening, but she felt helpless before them.

At lunch time, the kids were at the table arguing over who would get the last cookie. The baby was in his high chair playing "drop-the-spoon-and-watch-Mommy-pick-it-up." Just as the phone rang, Billy made a grab for the cookie and knocked over his milk, drenching Susie's lap. Susie broke out into gasping sobs, while the baby decided to add his lunch to the mess on the floor.

Something inside Nancy's head snapped. She felt a definite sensation of losing control. Trembling with rage, she grabbed Billy by the arm and swung him out of the chair. "Get a towel and clean this milk up! Susie, stop your sniveling. I can't stand it! And you," she rasped through clenched teeth at the baby, who by this time was loudly voicing his complaints, "I'm not going to pick up this mess one more time! I want you all to go to your rooms and not to come out till I say so! Move it! Now!"

The room fell into silence. Nancy stood frozen in

place, her face in her hands. An overwhelming sense of guilt and failure flooded over her, replacing the anger and bringing the emotional release of tears.

"Oh, Lord Jesus, help me! Only You know how close I came to hitting them. If I had started, I don't know if I would have been able to stop. You know how much I love my children . . . but at that moment I felt such anger and resentment. Oh, God, help me. Please help!"

Every mother can relate to Nancy's situation, for what parent hasn't faced moments when the demands of the family seem more than he or she can handle? Unfortunately, some parents are not able to resist the temptation to vent their suppressed hostility on their children. I am sure no parent sets out to purposely hurt his child, but as Nancy said, once you start it's hard to stop. Nearly ten million child abuse cases come before our courts each year. Thousands of children are literally beaten to death, victims of their parents' misdirected and uncontrolled hostility. Countless others survive, physically and emotionally damaged for life. Most will probably inflict their own pain and rage on their friends, their mates, and later on their own children.

Hostility has infected the home in other ways. Statistics indicate that one out of four families in the United States is touched by incest. You would be amazed at the number of women who write or come to me with similar stories. "Brother Sumrall, the first person who ever sexually attacked me was my father. He would send my mother out for something, just so he could lay with me. He told me he would kill me if I told. Now I have a husband and children of my own, and I am still so angry inside!"

Ephesians 6:4 says, "Ye fathers, provoke not your children to wrath: but bring them up in the nurture and admonition of the Lord."

Keith Miller tells the touching story of a former pro athlete who finally got tired of rebelling against God and decided to make an all-out commitment to Jesus. Almost immediately, his family saw him change from a hostile, belligerent tyrant to a man who honestly wanted to love and take care of them. He began spending time with his children and openly communicating with his wife.

About two weeks later his twelve-year-old son came in to talk to him. This boy had no friends at school and had begun to steal things from around the neighborhood to get attention. He was almost totally alone. "Dad," he said hesitantly, "what's happened to you lately?" His dad (who had been a tough professional athlete) looked up from his desk. "Well, son," he struggled for the right words, "I—guess I was making a pretty big mess out of my life and I decided I'd ask God to take it over and show me how to live it."

The boy looked at him and then down at the floor. "Dad," he said quietly, "I think I'd like to do that too."

The father just stood there with tears running down his cheeks and he and the boy held each other and wept together. The next day Jack had to go to New York on a business trip for two weeks. On the way back he was anxious to get home. When his plane got in, his son broke through the crowd and ran out on the ramp to meet his father. His eyes were shining with excitement! Hugging him, he said breathlessly, in a kind of grateful wonder, "Daddy, do you know what God has done?"

"No, what son?" his dad asked.

"He's changed every kid in my class!!"[2]

Children model themselves after the examples we set before them. The home is the perfect place for children to learn to handle their feelings in a healthy way—to learn gentleness, kindness, forgiveness, and unselfishness. It is also where the opposite is easily learned.

I was sitting on the front porch of a pastor's home one afternoon, and a sweet-faced little neighbor girl of five or six came over and sat down with me. She looked up at me and said in a matter-of-fact voice, "I'm going to kill you."

I reacted as though she had said she was going to kiss me. "That's very sweet of you. Who did you hear say that?"

"That's what my daddy told my mama a while ago," she replied.

"Yes," I sighed, "that's what I thought."

It is by such careless words that seeds of hostility are sown into the fertile soil of our children's minds and hearts. How easily are the sins of a parent perpetuated in his child!

It is a foolish person who transmits hostility from generation to generation.

The Green-Eyed Monster and Hostility

Jealousy has been called a "green-eyed monster," and rightly so. It is an insidious thing, born out of our

28

discontentment with who we are or what we have.

A very good friend of mine said that a Christian competitor of his was doing so well with his business that he found it difficult to speak peaceably about him when anyone mentioned his name. They were both building contractors, and one was building more houses than the other.

My friend finally prayed, "Lord, I don't dislike this man. We are friends. We belong to the same clubs and attend the same church. But every time his name is mentioned I say something negative about him. I don't like it in myself, and I want to quit."

"Do you?" the Lord gently challenged.

"Yes, I really do," my friend answered.

"All right," the Lord said. "Every time you say something negative about him, send him a twenty-five-dollar check as a gift."

You would be amazed at how quickly my friend learned to say good things about that gentleman when it was costing him twenty-five dollars every time he let his jealousy control his tongue.

Proverbs 10:12 says, "Hatred stirreth up strifes: but love covereth all sins."

Hatred and resentment are common producers of hostility. There is nothing more difficult for most people than forgiving someone who has hurt or persecuted them. And yet we have only to look at the lives and attitudes of saints such as Corrie ten Boom, who have been the objects of naked, unrestrained brutality, to see that forgiveness is possible through the power of God.

John Perkins, the founder of Voice of Calvary Ministries, was another such victim of blind hate and prejudice. As a black pastor in Mississippi in the late 1960s and early 1970s, he felt called to speak out in favor of the civil rights movement that was sweeping through the South, triggering fear and hostility in those who resented the inevitable changes. As a result, Perkins was put in jail and nearly beaten to death. The following is part of the testimony of a fellow victim.

> [The sheriffs] had a leather blackjack thing and they began beating on Reverend Brown, Reverend Perkins, David Nall, and myself . . . they beat Rev. Brown down to the floor and then Rev. Perkins was dragged over on the other side and beaten down by about five other officers. I could hear them being beaten and then I was knocked out and when I came to I heard them ordering Rev. Perkins to mop up the blood that was on the floor and Rev. Perkins was lying sorta stunned on the floor and they kicked him until he got up. . . . then Sheriff E. and two or three patrol officers would walk by every two or three minutes and kick or hit Rev. Perkins with one of their blackjacks or their feet.[3]

Most of us find it impossible to understand the intensity of hatred and disregard for human dignity that allows such violence. It is even more inconceivable that someone could live through such an ordeal without coming away bitter and full of anger. But here again, God's power protected a man from being infected by the hate and hostility of those who persecuted him. Perkins concludes the retelling of the nightmare.

> They were like savages—like some horror out of the night. And I can't forget their faces, so twisted with hate. It was like looking at white-faced demons. Hate did that to them. . . .

But you know, I couldn't hate back. When I saw what hate had done to them, I couldn't hate back. I could only pity them. I didn't ever want hate to do to me what it had done to those men.[4]

The potential destructive power of bitterness and the hate that is its direct descendant is greater than any other negative human emotion. And God will not tolerate it in His children. Dr. Jack Hayford explains:

God refuses to raise a breed of sons and daughters who are unlike Him. He has sired us. He insists that every latent trait of our former heritage, as offspring of Adam's race, be wormed out of us. He won't allow unforgiveness to continue. It's not in His nature, so He confronts it in ours.[5]

Hostility and Prejudice

Fear, misunderstanding, and ignorance often create hostility and another closely related feeling—prejudice. In the jungles of Ecuador a few years ago, a group of missionaries were murdered by a tribe of Indians who had been convinced by their leader that the white-skinned outsiders were a threat. Racial and language barriers prevented communication that could have explained the missionaries' presence and put the tribesmen's fear to rest.

Some time later, the message of the gospel was preached to these people, and many responded. Today, many of these Indians serve the Lord by spreading the good news to others who still live in the darkness of their ignorance and fear.

Fear and Misunderstanding

Fear and misunderstanding produce a vicious cycle. What we don't understand, we fear; what we fear, we don't take time to understand.

Lack of self-esteem leaves one vulnerable to anger and hostility. A person who can express his anger in a positive, thoughtful way likes himself better than someone who hurts himself or others. A low self-image also makes one more sensitive to criticism, more easily hurt or angered.

Fear of rejection causes a hostile reaction. When we feel rejected, we in turn reject others. Being ignored as though we don't exist or being treated as though we are worthless can produce an instinctive, spontaneous reaction of anger. In this instance, the anger is a demand that our value as people be recognized.

Feelings of uselessness or of not being wanted or needed can produce deep hostility. This is a common problem among the elderly, who are often forced to retire not only from their jobs but also from active participation in other areas as well. Many become cranky and irritable, driving people away, when what they want and need is to be accepted back into the ranks of responsible adults who have something of value to contribute.

Dependency, or the fear of becoming dependent upon a person or a relationship, can illicit angry, hostile behavior. Many people today have become obsessed with false concepts of freedom, individuality, and self-gratification that twenty years ago would have been more rightly labeled irresponsibility, self-centeredness, and selfishness. This concern for "me, myself, and I'' has spawned a growing disdain for commitment in relationships. People don't want to get involved because involvement costs. ''Non-involvement, however, creates an emptiness and hostility that are much harder to handle,'' writes Elizabeth Skoglund in her book, *To Anger, With Love.*[6]

Skoglund continues:

> Besides the frustration and anger created by fluctuating social values many people also experience inner hostility that is derived from a sense of rootlessness. This is partially the result of value conflict, but it is also due to the increased isolation of the individual in our society (and this affects Christians too). . . .

> Perhaps a feeling of meaninglessness is related to all the reasons for anger in our society. An increasing number of people seek psychological help because they are bored. Many of the very young feel an apathy toward life that promotes feelings of hostility as well as destructive behavior. . . . Extremes of individualism contribute to boredom because meaning can be found only in [committed] relationships. Value changes and rootlessness make a person wonder what life is all about, and even the Christian, who is sure of his or her eternal destiny, may question the how and why of now.[7]

Resentment's Poison

Resentment and bitterness go hand in hand with hostility. When we resent a painful or difficult happening in our lives, such as the death of a loved one or a sickness or the loss of a job, we soon find ourselves growing bitter, no longer able to take pleasure in all the good things God has blessed us with. We strike out at family and friends, unaware of the way bitterness has poisoned our thinking and relationships.

The resentful person stands to be hurt the most by nursing his grudge. As we relive in our thinking whatever it was that caused us to become hostile, we allow the poison of these undesirable feelings to endanger even our health. Many physical problems that have no physiological cause are directly related to what is going on in our heads—unresolved problems, anger, and hurts (real or imagined).

We need to read and reread 1 Corinthians 13 often. In verse 5 we are told that love "doth not behave itself unseemly, seeketh not her own, is not easily provoked, thinketh no evil."

How we need to learn these godly principles and make them a part of our everyday experience! What grief and anguish we would spare ourselves if we consciously practiced these admonitions meant for our own good!

Resentment usually gives way to vengeance, as we plot ways to get even with someone we feel has wronged us. How quickly we forget Romans 12:19:

> . . . avenge not yourselves, but rather give place unto wrath: for it is written, Vengeance is mine; I will repay, saith the Lord.

What is the answer for the person who struggles with resentment and bitterness? The counsel of the Word stands sure:

> Let all bitterness, and wrath, and anger, and clamor, and evil speaking, be put away from you, with all

malice: And be ye kind one to another, tenderhearted, forgiving one another, even as God for Christ's sake hath forgiven you (Eph. 4:31,32).

We must guard our thought lives. Philippians 4:8 lists preventive measures the Christian can employ:

Finally, brethren, whatsoever things are true, whatsoever things are honest, whatsoever things are just, whatsoever things are pure, whatsoever things are lovely, whatsoever things are of good report; if there be any virtue, and if there be any praise, think on these things.

The promise is that if we do this, the God of peace will be with us (see v. 9).

Recently some friends traveled from Michigan to Indiana to hear me speak. I was surprised and pleased to see them in the congregation, until they came up to speak to me after the service. They explained that they had come to confess the great bitterness and hostility they had felt for me and to ask my forgiveness.

I smiled in amazement. "That's a real revelation to me. I always thought you were some of my best friends!"

"No, we have not been your friends," they replied. "We have spoken badly about you behind your back."

I forgave them, and they left with peace restored to their hearts. To this day I do not know what caused such deep bitterness in those people, but I learned long ago the wisdom of not reacting to another's pain and weakness out of my own.

There is a story about John Wesley walking down a path and meeting a man who hated him because of his preaching. The man stood astride of the walk, saying, "I won't get out of the way for a fool."

John Wesley stepped aside. "Sir, I will," he said, letting the man pass. We must refuse to be a part of another person's hostility.

Hostile Humor

We must also be careful how we speak to other people. Hostile teasing or belittling can generate tremendous hostility. This is particularly a problem between husbands and wives. It is often tempting to point out an irritating flaw by way of a teasing remark, or to retaliate for past hurts by making a spouse look foolish in front of others.

One time I was in Alaska, staying in the home of a man who had gone there in search of gold. He had found an Eskimo wife, and had become the town's postmaster.

They had a quarrel. She said something in broken English and he responded with, "*Squaw*, you shut up!"

Her immediate shame and embarrassment were painfully obvious. He had deliberately belittled her in front of us by calling her a squaw instead of his wife. I still chuckle when I picture the infuriated little Eskimo woman's retort: "White woman good enough for you. Eskimo woman *too* good!"

When you belittle a person you attack the most vulnerable, intimate part of his psyche—his sense of self-worth. Hostility is an inevitable result.

Finally, sin and feelings of conviction over sin in

one's life can cause tremendous hostility. A Chicago newspaper reported the story of a Christian father who went to see his son in prison. Heartbroken over his son's condition, the man asked him to give his heart to Jesus. Before the prison guards could stop him, the boy had beaten his father to the ground with his fists and walked off cursing. The son was under conviction for his sins and he vented the resulting hostility upon his godly father, who wanted to see him saved and released from his terrible bondage of guilt.

Sadly, hostility hurts no one more than those who allow it to take root in their lives.

Chapter 3

THE EFFECTS OF HOSTILITY

Our world is destroying itself through hostility. Wars ravage the land and kill the innocent. Racism fills our hearts with blind hate and turns neighbor against neighbor. The world's religions continue their contest for control of men's hearts and minds, while we in the body of Christ are robbed of our strength of unity by our own internal bickering.

Hostility eats away at the foundations of relationships, businesses, governments, and whole civilizations. Some historians believe that the great city of Athens, which dominated the world intellectually for hundreds of years, died internally from hostility. Everybody was angry at somebody. Everybody was suing somebody. The army couldn't win a battle because they were too busy fighting each other to fight the enemy effectively. By the time they were conquered, the Athenians were nearly unconscious from internal feuding. They had literally destroyed themselves before the enemy ever attacked.

America today is in a frighteningly similar situation. We're so full of hostility towards one another that it takes a terrible tragedy or serious threat to remind us that we must stand and work together to survive. We need one another, both individually and collectively, and if we don't determine to put our differences aside and reverse the deteriorating effects of hostility in our land, our society may suffer the same ending Athens did.

Irrational Hostility

Our court systems are booked years in advance, not only with criminal cases but with the petty grievances of friends and even family members who will not forgive and forget.

I read in the newspaper about two friends who were playing tennis together. One of them was inadvertently hit by the ball and received a black eye. Outraged, he took his opponent to court. The judge dismissed the case, saying, "You cannot sue a man for hitting a ball you happened to get in the way of."

The hearing of nonsensical cases such as this one costs taxpayers thousands of dollars each year. Worse, it keeps our courts from settling far more important problems in a timely manner.

Hostility has a crippling effect on the human personality. Joy, peace of mind, contentment, and rational thinking are replaced by hatred, vindictive thoughts, discontentment, and a general confusion. The Hebrew Talmud says, "As a man gets angry, he falls into error." Hostility clouds our thinking and leaves us vulnerable to all sorts of erroneous teachings and ideas.

Demonic Deception

The most reasonable of men becomes unpredictable and even dangerous in the grip of hostile emotions. His whole personality may change radically. He may be soft-spoken and apparently in control of his actions one moment, cruel, violent, and vindictive the next. Wife-beating, child abuse, and other acts of violence are generally the result of uncontrolled hostility.

When the full force of that emotional negativism is directed toward oneself, it gradually destroys the essential element of hope within the human heart, eating away at natural instincts of self-preservation, until suicide seems to offer a blessed relief from a life of pain and unresolved problems.

"It has been said that suicide is Satan's gateway to defeat, but Christ is the only Door to freedom and victory,"[1] writes Helen Hosier. According to her book *Suicide, A Cry For Help,* suicide is the second leading cause of death among young people between the ages of fifteen and twenty-four. But it also takes its tragic toll on children as young as six and seven years old, on the middle-aged, and on the elderly. Neither money, fame, nor success can immunize us from an inner sense of worthlessness and helplessness that produces despair.

Paul said that unless a person receives help from others that can instill some hope within him, he may be "swallowed up with overmuch sorrow" (2 Cor. 2:7).

Unless we are willing to do this, Satan will get the advantage. Those are not my words; again they come from Paul (2 Cor. 2:11). Bitterness and discouragement can so overtake one that unless we who are strong in the Lord and aware of the adversary's tactics come to the rescue of one who is overburdened with life's complexities, there is great danger that such a person will not recover, but will succumb to despair. It is in these moments that mental derangement can take over to the extent that even a committed Christian can commit suicide.

The final act of suicide is basically a resolution, a movement, perceived as the only possible way out of a life situation felt to be unbearable by one of low sense of competence, with hope extinguished.[2]

Hostility opens the door to the most demonic kind of deception, and often blinds us to the simplest truths.

Habitual Hostility

Hostility destroys human potential and hinders productivity. The habitually hostile person is hard to teach, to work with, or to live with. His anger constantly gets in the way of personal growth, causing him to be impatient and less careful than he might otherwise be. Automobile accidents are often the result of drivers allowing their anger to take control of their steering wheels. And studies show that eighty to

41

ninety percent of industrial accidents happen to only ten percent of the workers. This is generally not attributed to a lack of skill on the job, but to a characteristic of aggression in certain personalities.

Although there is no doubt that hostility generates a certain amount of energy, it is usually an undisciplined energy that hinders more than helps. For this reason, professional athletes have learned to manifest less hostility than amateurs might show. Experience has taught them that hostility toward opponents or teammates usually ends in unnecessary errors.

Hostility puts people in prisons, hospitals, and insane asylums. It confuses issues, making it difficult to keep priorities in a healthy order.

The suppressed anger and hurt that leads to hostility tears families apart and destroys friendships by short-circuiting communication. Alan Loy McGinnis observes this in his book *The Friendship Factor.*

> When passively hostile people blow, their expression of anger is disproportionate to the complaint because they are really ventilating a lot of past grievances all at once. The result is that communication shorts out.[3]

The Robber

Hostility isolates people in a world of "self." Since the one relating to a hostile person never knows when the wrong word or look is going to illicit a violent or cutting response, openness and honesty in the relationship are gradually replaced by a spirit of fear.

In a wider sense, this spirit of fear hangs like a pall

over the earth, keeping us on guard and slightly uneasy whenever we're in unfamiliar territory. No longer do we assume the best of people. Instead, we expect the worst, and anything else is a pleasant surprise! No longer do we face the world with positive expectation and trust, but with skepticism and a "prove-it-to-me" attitude. Hostility takes away our spontaneity and places limitations on our human potential. It is a robber.

Hostility has invaded the classroom, making it difficult for our children to obtain a good education.

Dr. Kenneth L. Fish found rebellion and hostility in the schools so disturbing that he did extensive research in this area. His book *Conflict and Dissent in the High School* makes this statement:

> High school walkouts, sit-ins, and school closings . . . interfere with the regular course of learning; they complicate the already critical job of staffing schools with good teachers, and they are one more symptom of the disintegrative processes which threaten American society.[4]

It has also been observed that learning difficulties are seldom due to lack of intelligence. Often, a child's hostility toward his teacher stifles his motivation to learn. This was true of Albert Einstein. His schoolwork was so poor that his teachers and parents feared he was retarded. The headmaster of his school is quoted as saying, "He'll never make a success at anything!" However, it was hostile defiance against his teachers, not lack of ability, that caused Einstein's poor grades.

Young people's rebellion against authority has unfortunately caused more damage than a few failing grades. Dr. Milton Layden observes in *Escaping the Hostility Trap* that drug abuse is also directly linked to hostility.

> The principal reason a youngster starts taking drugs is his hostile feeling toward established authority. In a study involving hundreds of high school students, more of those who were exposed to drug information (its negative effects) became users than those who were not given any information at all. When an authority-hating youngster is warned of the dire consequences of drug abuse, he may start taking the drug as a means of defiance.[5]

It is also a proven fact that hostility is responsible for a number of other physical and emotional illnesses.

Insomnia

According to medical authorities, insomnia is often the direct result of suppressed hostility toward a close associate (spouse, boss, friend). The unresolved hostility causes the brain to generate anxiety at an abnormally high level, which makes relaxation and sleep extremely difficult.

Ulcers

Ulcers also can be a physical manifestation of hostility. You can tell that your stomach is reacting to negative emotion if you experience what feels like butterflies or a knot in your stomach. What you are feeling is not an illusion; experiments have shown that the "knot" actually exists. A patient was placed in front of an X-ray machine and antagonized; his stomach literally began to knot up as his irritation grew.

Headaches

It is estimated that about ten million people a year seek medical help for persistent headaches. While medical science knows relatively little about the cause of headaches, Dr. Milton Layden of Johns Hopkins Hospital observed that ninety percent of the patients he treated for migraine headache found relief from their excruciating pain by getting rid of suppressed hostility (see his book *Escaping the Hostility Trap*).

Heart Attacks

More people die from heart attacks and circulatory disease than from any other illness. Many die suddenly, without previous symptoms. Many specialists in heart disease believe that stress is the greatest factor in producing heart attacks, and nothing creates more stress within the human soul than hostility.

Obesity, Alcoholism, Gambling, Infidelity

Because their hostility prevents them from receiving the love and affirmation of those around them, hostile

45

people may turn to other sources for pleasure, comfort, and a sense of self-worth. For some, alcohol, drugs, gambling, or extramarital sex temporarily fill the void. For others who shun these outlets, eating is the most accessible pleasure.

The late Walter Trobisch, well-known counselor, lecturer, and writer, stressed in his book *Love Yourself* that the lack of self-love creates an empty hole. Overeating or getting drunk are futile attempts to fill this empty hole. This is hostility directed inward to punish the unloved self.

Fatigue, Hypertension, Nervous Breakdowns

Fatigue, hypertension, nervous breakdowns, high blood pressure, and even cancer can be the result of hostility—which in reality is nothing more than unconfessed sin in our lives. Often medical science cannot find the cause of an illness because the problem is spiritual, not physical. For many problems, the only effective medicine is the cleansing, healing blood of Jesus applied to broken, sin-infested lives.

Here again, hostility, or rather our unwillingness to confess our hostility and forgive others, has the power to prevent us from grabbing hold of the one sure weapon within our reach. When we approach God in prayer, we must do so in accordance with the rules He has set forth in His Word.

Therefore if thou bring thy gift to the altar, and there rememberest that thy brother hath ought against thee;
Leave there thy gift before the altar, and go thy way;

first be reconciled to thy brother, and then come and offer thy gift (Matt. 5:23,24).

As far as God is concerned, right relationships take precedence over worship and prayer. He has told us that we are to forgive others as He, for His Son's sake, has forgiven us. As long as we cannot find it in ourselves to relinquish our anger, bitterness, resentment, or hurt feelings, God will not receive our praise or release His flow of healing grace into our lives.

Chapter 4

THE MIND AND HOSTILITY

Hostility does not spring full grown out of nowhere to suddenly take control of our lives. It begins as a seed of anger, resentment, or bitterness planted in the inner recesses of our minds. If not weeded out, it takes root and draws nourishment from undisciplined thoughts, negative attitudes, and other sin in our lives. Soon it becomes a motivating force, warping our logic, influencing our actions, and dictating our responses to others.

The Real Battle

Proverbs 23:7 says, "For as he thinketh in his heart, so is he: Eat and drink, saith he to thee; but his heart is not with thee."

Our heart attitude and thought life are very closely related. What a man thinks in his heart determines what he is. Therefore, although our battle against hostility is a spiritual one, the battleground is the mind and the weapons are ideas and thoughts.

> Having made peace through the blood of his cross, by him to reconcile all things unto himself; by him, I say, whether they be things in earth, or things in heaven. And you, that were sometime alienated and enemies in *your mind* by wicked works, yet now hath he reconciled (Col. 1:20,21, italics added).

Since the mind is the key to the personality, there is a continuous battle going on for control of our thought lives. We are constantly exposed to the subtle campaign of the enemy through certain movies, television shows, magazines, books, and music that portray ungodly and hostile behavior as natural and healthy. Sin and perversion have been redefined and reclassified as "personal freedoms," and we are accused of having closed minds and being bigots if we dare call sin "sin."

In Romans 8:7 we are told that "the carnal mind is enmity against God . . . ," and 1 Peter 1:13 urges believers to "gird up the loins of your mind . . ." against the propaganda of unrighteousness.

Philippians 2:5 instructs us to "Let this mind be in you, which was also in Christ Jesus." This mental transformation cannot take place if our relationship with Christ only includes attending church on Sunday and saying "grace" at mealtimes. We must spend time getting to know Him through His Word and through meaningful conversations in prayer.

It is also a fact of life that we are influenced by our environment. Our friends and families have a tremendous influence upon our attitudes and thinking.

49

Peer pressure is especially hard for the young to resist. I know from experience.

I grew up angry. I can't tell you why. I had a good home, and I believe God gave me a good mind. But I was caught up in a spirit of rebellion that dominated all my close friends. We fed one another's anger and dissatisfaction and shaped one another's thoughts to conform to our own hostility. I was a rebel on my way into an eternity without God.

Then I contracted tuberculosis. It was the best thing that could have happened to me. I lay in bed for five months, and not once did the gang come to see me. I realized how shallow and meaningless our relationships were and how confused my thinking had been.

When I was finally up and around again, my friends suddenly reappeared, wanting to pick up where we had left off. "No," I told them, "You didn't want to see me when I was sick. I don't want to see you now that I'm well." I was finally free to think my own thoughts and make my own decisions.

Interpersonal Relationships

If our minds tell us we are not being treated as well as someone else, or that someone else is more talented or capable, we are open to resentment, envy, or feelings of inadequacy—all of which can lead to hostility.

The mind is constantly evaluating other people's behavior as acceptable or unacceptable, and we respond accordingly. This is how we often get into trouble. Since we cannot possibly read another's mind or heart, we cannot know their needs or problems. Thus we make judgments based upon appearances, not fact.

My wife went to the post office one day to pick up our office mail. She greeted the postal clerk with a cheerful, "Good morning. How are you today?"

He just grunted.

The next day she returned and was helped by the same man. Again she greeted him with, "Good morning. It's a beautiful day, isn't it? How are you?"

No response.

The third morning the man was again sullen and unfriendly, and my wife began praying for him. By Friday she walked into the post office determined to be friendly, in spite of what she now considered the man's ungracious and unfriendly attitude. Instead, before she could say a word, the clerk leaned across the counter and said in a broken voice, "Mrs. Sumrall, I am sorry for the way I've behaved these last few days, but my wife died two weeks ago and I just can't get over it. I am the saddest person in the world."

Immediately my wife saw that it wasn't this man's nature to be surly and unpleasant. He had received a crushing blow and was still staggering from its impact. His attitude reflected his misery, and her conclusions about his personality had been mistaken.

So often it is the pain in us reacting to the pain in someone else that creates hostility. If we could only withhold judgment and table our response until we are sure we have the whole picture, a lot of unnecessary hurt and anger could be avoided. Instead, the human mind calls for immediate sympathy and understanding, and when it doesn't get it, it often strikes back without thinking things through or trying to see the other person's point of view.

Our thinking is also influenced by associations. The mind links a current situation with something from the past and draws a conclusion that can be completely erroneous and misleading.

A few years ago I traveled into the Grand Chaco Boreano in Paraguay. We went by river as far as the boat could take us, then traveled by horseback for several miles. When we reached the area where the most primitive Indians lived, my interpreter said to me, "I must warn you not to use the word 'Christian' around these people. They might cut your throat."

Astounded, I asked him why.

He explained that the Paraguayan army had caused these people great trouble and pain—rounding them up like animals to move them from place to place, telling them what they could and could not do, and even shooting them down in cold blood. The Paraguayans were Catholics. The Indians had seen them hold mass and believed that they were Christians. So they associated the word "Christian" with those soldiers, and probably would kill anyone who claimed to be one. A beautiful word had been made repulsive and hateful through association.

"What word do I use instead?" I asked.

My interpreter answered, "Ask them to become a 'creyente,' a believer. After they are 'creyentes,' then you can explain that the word 'Christian' is not related to the army, or to guns and killing, but to life and love through Jesus Christ."

Think Before You Speak

Many times we would be wise to think carefully before we speak. A word may mean one thing to us but something entirely different to someone else. We also need to be careful how we use words to manipulate others. Parents are often guilty of using verbal threats and misinformation to control a child's behavior without giving proper thought to the indelible impressions they are making on young minds.

A friend of mine, Glen Johnson, is a missionary to Alaska. His work takes him to remote villages where white men are seldom seen. Arriving at one village with candy and little toys to hand out to the children, he was dismayed to see the little ones run screaming in terror to hide from him. Asking some Eskimo fathers why the children ran, he was told with a laugh, "It is because we tell them if they are bad we will give them to the white man, who will take them far away."

The fathers' thoughtless threats had created a deep fear in the children's hearts, making it impossible for them to receive Glen's offerings of friendship. That fear might well develop into a suspicion and hostility toward all foreigners in years to come. Parents should not instill unfounded fears to control a child's behavior.

(Lying tactics such as this are as effective on adults as they are on children. Satan is a master of deceit. He plays on our imagination with fears of what might be and with fantasies of impending danger. Our own insecurities do the rest. Before we know it, we are behaving as if our fears are fact and the danger a reality.)

This same thoughtlessness can result in an insensitivity to other people's feelings, which can cause them to react with hostility. Shortly after I was married, a painful incident showed me how thoughtless and insensitive I could be.

Before my marriage, I traveled all over the world. During that time I heard lots of ethnic jokes. One night I attempted to amuse my in-laws by observing that throughout their history the British had proved themselves the bravest of soldiers. They had always fought to the last *Frenchman.*

It was an innocent little joke that would have been perfectly acceptable and inoffensive in the United States, but my wife's family are proud British Canadians. My father-in-law, a military man from way back, stood to his feet and exclaimed, "You can't say that kind of thing in my home!"

My thoughtless remark had offended rather than amused, and I learned the wisdom of forgetting jokes that buy laughter at the expense of someone else's dignity.

The Battle of the Mind

The human mind is a computer-like storage system of knowledge, past experiences, and learned responses. From the day we are born our "response systems" are being programmed. When a small child reaches out to touch the "pretty baby" reflected in the shiny side of a toaster, Mama yells "Hot!" and he learns that "hot" means "Hurt. Don't touch."

The same is true of much more complicated emotional responses. When we have a painful or frightening experience, the next time a similar situation occurs we unconsciously prepare to be hurt or frightened again. Of course, much of this habitual response is healthy and works to our advantage as we learn from past mistakes. It is only when we become locked into behavior that is unloving or unproductive that we must stop and take stock.

We give in to impatience, anger, or resentment on one occasion and soon this becomes a way of life. The worst part is that often we accept these negative personality traits as part of our "natural makeup." "Oh, he just has a short fuse," we say of the man who can't seem to control his temper. Or we excuse someone's behavior by explaining, "She can't help being demanding; she's a perfectionist." Such people continue to be critical and impatient, and we really haven't done them a favor. It's much easier to blame emotional self-indulgence on "Mother Nature" than to recognize it as sin and submit it to the transforming discipline of the Holy Spirit.

> . . . put off concerning the former conversation the old man, which is corrupt according to the deceitful lusts; And be renewed in the spirit of your mind; And that ye put on the new man, which after God is created in righteousness and true holiness (Eph. 4:22–24).

The transformation from "old man" to "new man" is not automatic when we receive Christ. It is a result of our active obedience to the Scripture's admonition to "put off" or consciously reject the old life-style, to "be renewed" in our minds through prayer and the study of God's Word, and to "put on" the new image of Christlike behavior and attitudes. Again, the battle is in the mind; it has to do with the will.

The first step in accomplishing this radical change is to realize that none of us needs to be permanently enslaved to old emotional habits. Our minds are constantly making value judgments, deciding if something is good, bad, pleasant, or painful. We may have little control over our immediate emotional reaction to these things, but with the help of the Holy Spirit we can control our outward responses.

Both the world and the Bible agree that the "computer" can be reprogrammed. The world offers many different kinds of programs of self-analysis and mind control to achieve this end. Books have been written on the importance of controlling situations and not allowing situations to control us. We must learn to *act*, not *react*. One way to avoid hostile, negative confrontations, we are told by Theodora Wells in *Keeping Your Cool Under Fire,* is to learn to communicate nondefensively.

> Learning to communicate non-defensively is easier said than done. It involves looking at some of your own attitudes, inner rules, and underlying beliefs that may contribute to feelings of defensiveness. In the process of becoming non-defensive you are also in the process of becoming more of your own person. . . . As you exercise more choices, you will be redefining yourself, renegotiating your relationships, and revising the results you get.[1]

It's not bad advice, as far as it goes. In essence, the writer is telling us to stop reacting with a preprogrammed response every time someone hits a certain emotional key. But even Wells admits that breaking that habit by sheer human determination is difficult at best.

Christians have a far more effective resource to draw from, found in Galatians 2:20.

> I am crucified with Christ: nevertheless I live; yet not I, but Christ liveth in me: and the life which I now live in the flesh I live by the faith of the Son of God, who loved me, and gave himself for me.

Christ living in me means I am no longer bound by old thought patterns or habitual responses. My life is no longer ruled by the old sin nature, but by God's love and mercy and His empowering Spirit.

The apostle Paul had a wonderful, practical understanding of this truth. Helen Hosier explains this in her book *It Feels Good to Forgive.*

> Paul knew what it meant to be mistreated by those who claimed to be brothers in Christ. But he submerged his hostility by saturating himself with thoughts of the forgiveness and love of Christ. It worked every time. Paul speaks from bitter experience. His word to us is that we too can have strength for all things in Christ who empowers us. . . .[2]

Chapter 5

HOSTILITY TOWARDS GOD AND GOD'S CHILDREN

The Father-heart of God must be grieved when He sees hostility among His children. Nothing creates more confusion and turmoil within the human heart than hostility (usually suppressed or redirected) towards God. Both of these forms of hostility have far-reaching implications that affect both our individual spiritual growth and the effectiveness of our ministry to others.

We Are Being Watched

The world is watching us. We are "living epistles," being read by men. The apostle Paul talks of this in his second letter to the Christians in Corinth (see 2 Cor. 3:2).

Our lives either verify or nullify the reality of what

we profess to believe. Words are cheap. But disciplined, loving actions are priceless and more powerful than any sermon or theological debate.

Proverbs 21:14 says, "A gift in secret pacifieth anger. . . ." To love those who are unlovely—those who malign our good names, who show none of the fruits of the Spirit—that is a great challenge. We cannot succeed if we are harboring anger and resentment. This can curdle our spirits.

Jesus: Our Example

In John 17:21, with the agony of the cross within hours of becoming a reality, Jesus' prayer to the Father was "That they all may be one; as thou, Father, art in me, and I in thee, that they also may be one in us: that the world may believe that thou hast sent me."

Jesus knew that the significance of what He was to endure would be best communicated by the living witness of those whose lives had already been touched by His saving grace, and that the burden of proof to the nonbelievers would lie upon the shoulders of His followers. If the world saw a community of believers truly united in love—edifying, serving, and lifting one another up—able to accept one another's differences while still functioning with one mind, one heart, and one purpose, they would not be able to resist the power of such a testimony.

And indeed, Acts 4:32 indicates just such a oneness within the early church: "And the multitude of them that believed were of one heart and of one soul. . . ."

Contentious Children

We encounter contentious Christians in the Corinthian church. The Corinthian problem was one of divisions among the brethren. Paul addressed himself to the problem in his first letter to them. The genius of the apostle is clearly seen as his feelings spill over. One can sense the spirit that prompted him to immediately confront these Christians with what had come to his attention:

> Now I beseech you, brethren, by the name of our Lord Jesus Christ, that ye all speak the same thing, and that there be no divisions among you; but that ye be perfectly joined together in the same mind and in the same judgment.
>
> For it hath been declared unto me of you, my brethren, by them which are of the house of Chloe, that there are contentions among you (1 Cor. 1:10,11).

Actually, the entire letter takes off at this point, speaking against being divided and about what it is that contributes to such hostility. Through it all one senses the sorrow Paul felt as he poured out his heart, calling for them to abandon their contentious spirit and to walk in the way of love. All of this leads up to 1 Corinthians 13, that great chapter on love. But its writing was prompted by ill will among the members of the body of Christ in that church.

Today we sing "They will know we are Christians by our love," and at the same time we harbor hostility and resentment against other members of the family of God for one reason or another. If Paul were to come

60

into our midst surely he would proclaim with the apostle James, ". . . My brethren, these things ought not so to be" (James 3:10).

How much we need to hear that message today!

This division in the body of Christ has presented the world with a tragic and seemingly irreparable fragmentation that directly contradicts the biblical concept of unity and acceptance of each other in love.

Our internal hostilities and bickering have broadened and multiplied down through the generations, until the church itself is lifted up by some as an exemplification of division, not unity. According to Webster's dictionary, the word "schism" is best defined as a formal division in a religious body or church.

To countermine this unfortunate state of affairs, we must prayerfully keep our thoughts and emotions cleansed by the Word of God and be sensitive to the first signs of hostility or prejudice towards other parts of the church. This does not mean we must necessarily come to a place of total agreement, but we must learn to receive one another in love. We nip hostility in the bud when we accept another's right to be different.

Even those closest to Jesus when He walked this earth disagreed occasionally on the most appropriate ways of communicating the truth of what had happened to Christ. Personalities differed. Backgrounds differed. Some were still bound to Jewish traditionalism. In other words, even the disciples remained unique individuals, complete with their own set of strengths and weaknesses—which inevitably led to differences of opinion. Still, they recognized the sovereign work of God in each other's lives. They drew strength from one another, and their love for

Christ triumphed over their differences. Hostility didn't have a chance to survive long in such an atmosphere of mutual caring.

Satan's Strategy: Divide and Conquer

We must recognize that Satan's main strategy is to divide and conquer. Jesus said that every kingdom divided against itself is brought to desolation and that "every city or house divided against itself shall not stand" (Matt. 12:25).

Hostility against God's children robs us of strength and leaves us far more vulnerable to deception and spiritual attack than we would be if the circle of fellowship were unbroken.

A friend relates the story of Stonewall Jackson, who saw his men fighting among themselves over battle strategy. The general is said to have jumped into the argument, stating, "Remember, gentlemen, the enemy is over there," pointing in the direction of the battle. Likewise, how tragic it is for church members to fight each other while Satan gains victories over men's immortal souls.[1]

What About Negative Feelings?

But while negative emotions such as resentment and pride can cause major problems, this does not necessarily mean that Christians must deny or feel guilty about negative feelings. Instead, we must grab the opportunity to use the impetus and energy generated by such feelings to accomplish positive goals.

How is this possible? Well, anger, for example, can be translated into positive reactions such as endurance, strength of conviction, and repentance.

This kind of constructive rechanneling of negative emotional energy may appear to border on repression. But there is a significant difference. One is accomplished through self-determination, the other through Holy Spirit-empowered redirection.

Anger over our own sin or over someone else's destructive behavior is not only good but often essential to seeing wrongs righted or unhealthy behavior challenged and changed. Unfortunately, many Christians live with the misconception that anger is always an expression of our sinful nature and therefore something to be rightly suppressed. This is especially true of the anger we may occasionally feel towards God.

Anger Towards God

Yes, I know. Christians are never supposed to be angry with God. If we are, He may strike us down with a bolt of lightning or turn us into a pillar of salt! In reality, the Bible gives us a graphic illustration that seems to indicate the exact opposite.

We are familiar with the story of the prophet Jonah who rebelled against God's direction for his life. (God wanted him to warn the people of Nineveh of His imminent judgment and destruction unless they repented from their evil ways.) Jonah's disobedience caused him to end up in the belly of a big fish. After three days God caused the fish to vomit Jonah up onto dry land, and Jonah, who had experienced a decided change of heart, headed straight for Nineveh to deliver God's message. The result was a great spiritual revival as the entire city confessed its sins and sought God's mercy and forgiveness. And God spared them.

But instead of being overjoyed by the people's honest repentance, the Bible says that Jonah was displeased and very angry. He went outside the city and sat sulking under the shade of a gourd vine, complaining:

> . . . "This is exactly what I thought you'd do, Lord, when I was there in my own country and you first told me to come here. That's why I ran away to Tarshish. For I knew you were a gracious God, merciful, slow to get angry, and full of kindness; I knew how easily you could cancel your plans for destroying these people.
>
> "Please kill me, Lord; I'd rather be dead than alive [when nothing that I told them happens]."
>
> Then the Lord said, "Is it right to be *angry* about *this*?" (Jonah 4:2–4 TLB).

God was chiding Jonah for his selfish self-absorption, but there is nothing in His response to indicate that He was outraged by Jonah's uninhibited expression of his true feelings. Even as Jonah sat complaining and feeling sorry for himself God took pity on him, arranging for a vine to spring up and spread its leaves to shade him.

To think we can hide our anger from God by pretending it doesn't exist is ridiculous. We may be able to fool ourselves, but we can never fool Him. When something happens that hurts us deeply, we may direct our anger at the person or thing that hurt us. But underneath that hurt is the thought that since God is ultimately in control of everything, He *could* have done something to protect us.

In her book *The Hidden Riches of Secret Places* Hazel McAlister writes with soul-level honesty about her anger with God for letting her father die when she was fifteen.

> I buried my anger. It was buried so deep that eventually I forgot about it. I didn't even know it was there.
>
> Someone said, "We bury our feelings and they grow." Silently, stealthily, completely unknown to me, my anger grew. It colored everything I thought—especially spiritual things. It governed many of the things I did and caused me to make most of my mistakes.
>
> I know now that to be angry is to be disobedient. The natural outgrowth of disobedience is rebellion, and with rebellion comes an unclean heart, a wrong spirit, and ultimately more anger.[2]

Hazel learned the importance of being honest with God about her feelings—not for His benefit but for her own. It is only by our willingness to take those hidden negative feelings and hurts out of the darkness and expose them, ugly and painful as they may be, that true healing and redemption can take place.

> Even though God knows everything, we must talk to Him about the things that bother us in our hearts, and as we converse . . . with Him, we free Him to forgive our anger, our resentment, our bitterness, our self-imposed guilt, our attitudes, and our actions. They are all changed by the blood of His Son. God allows differ-

ent experiences to come into our lives to discipline us, to mold us, to make us, and shape us into His likeness.[3]

While it is true that God is all-knowing, still *we* must articulate our hurts and whatever it is that is contributing to our hostility. When we feel that God is dealing with us harshly, we would do well to remember that God disciplines us as sons (see Heb. 12:7); and although present chastening (problems, hurts, anxieties) is not joyous, the promise is that "afterward it yieldeth the peaceable fruit of righteousness" (Heb. 12:11). This peace is exactly the opposite of the hostility so often harbored in the human heart.

Chapter 6

DO-IT-YOURSELF KITS

There is a way which seemeth right unto a man, but
the end thereof are the ways of death (Prov. 14:12).

Getting rid of hostility should be no great problem if
we are to believe the scores of psychologists and be-
havioral experts who write books or glibly discuss
their latest theories on our favorite TV talk shows.
Each has a foolproof answer that they guarantee will
relieve us of our anger and frustration. But since no
two cures are alike, we must decide which emotional
"do-it-yourself kit" is best.

Make-A-New-Resolution Kit

One of the oldest and most time-honored is the
Make-a-New-Resolution Kit. The New Year's resolution
has become a tradition. The old year with all its fail-

ures is gone, and the new year looms ahead, clean and untouched. It's the perfect time to start that new diet or throw away that last pack of cigarettes or decide to stop being hostile.

The problem with this kit is that its success is totally dependent upon our ability to control urges and responses that past experience has proven we have little or no control over. The alcoholic who swears off the bottle on December 31 usually finds the strength of his resolve diminishing with every passing day, until his need for a drink overpowers his desire to stay sober.

The same is true of overeating, smoking, gambling, or any other habitual bondage—including hostility. The habit may be subdued for a short time by self-control, but sooner or later our hold will slip and the relief will have been purely temporary.

Vent-Your-Emotions Kit

Another common solution is the *Vent-Your-Emotions* or *Let-It-All-Hang-Out Kit.* Since emotional repression is the root of hostility, we are told that we are too inhibited in expressing our true feelings. As soon as we break that inhibition and honestly express ourselves, the theory goes, we will be happier and healthier.

Classes are held to teach people how to vent their emotions in a "healthy" way. They are encouraged to scream, cry, smash things, beat pillows, speak obscenities—in general, to forget what is acceptable or unacceptable behavior and get the venom out.

This new "honesty" of expression is encouraged in

everyday situations. "Say what you feel. Be spontaneous. If you're angry, express it."

Recently medical science has reevaluated its opinion of this kind of therapy. More often than not, the undisciplined and thoughtless expression of negative emotions only compounds the problem. Although we need to express our feelings in honest, positive ways, spewing out our anger or hate whenever we feel like it is not the anwer. It is like telling a person that the way to stop drinking is to get roaring drunk.

Dr. Layden describes it this way.

> No doubt it's possible to avoid much of the anxiety and tension of suppressed hostility by openly venting our feelings. . . . But what is a person to do? Blast his boss, wife, or child whenever he feels like it? . . . If you are the type that yells, fights, and argues whenever you feel irritated, it is unlikely that you'll be the victim of a premature heart attack. But most people vent their anger only with those they don't fear (spouse, children, employees).[1]

A friend of mine pulled into a crowded parking lot next to a mother with three young sons. The mother was obviously frazzled; her hair was in curlers and her expression told the story of a tired, put-upon woman fed up with her kids and with life in general. As she got out of the car, the woman was in the midst of a verbal tirade against one of her little boys.

"I can't stand it any more! From the day you were born you've done nothing but cause trouble. You can't do *anything* right. I just wish you'd get out of my life. Just leave me alone!"

As the woman stormed off toward the store, leaving

the little boys standing uncertainly by the car, my friend heard a small voice say, "Mommy, I'm sorry. I didn't mean to." After a slight hesitation, the boys hurried to catch up with their mother, and my friend couldn't resist calling after them, "She loves you!"

Venting your anger can cause you to lose your mate, child, job and sometimes your life. At the very least, you're going to have to suffer unpleasant consequences, since your expression of anger will antagonize its recipient, and you'll soon be angry again because of the hostility you receive in retaliation. . . .

The habitually hostile person becomes trapped in a vicious circle since the hostility he uses to protect himself only incites ever-increasing incidences of the behavior it was meant to protect him from.[2]

The Positive-Thinking Kit

Positive thinking is one of the more attractive kits on the market today, but it is not a new revelation.

Back in 1910, a French pharmacist, Emile Coue, treated nervous disorders by instructing his patients to "think positively." According to this form of therapy, all you have to do to overcome fear, lack of confidence, negativism, pessimism, and nervous symptoms is to tell yourself that you can. . . . Today [this form of therapy] is referred to as "positive thinking."

Not only does such advice fail to overcome inferiority, worry, depression, illness, and personal problems, it actually makes them worse, since the practice of positive thinking leads to suppression of hostility and anxiety and consequently increases the likelihood of personal failure and emotional and physical illness.[3]

The power of positive thinking alone can never release us from the bondage of hostility or make us successes in our spiritual lives. Only the power of God within us can make us positive people.

Change-of-Scenery Kit

Running away from our problems is categorized under the more acceptable *Change-of-Scenery Kit.* We are a society of constant change. If we don't like our job, we quit and find a new one. If we don't like our neighborhood, we move. If we don't like our spouse, we get a new one.

Is everything going wrong at once? Get away for a while. A change of scenery will do you good. Take a sixty-day cruise, and everything will seem different when you come home. The problem with this solution is that the minute you get on board, you are going to find people you don't like. You'll encounter a whole new set of irritations that produce hostility. You'll find it's not your mother-in-law who grates on your nerves, but the man in the next cabin who snores all night. It's not your boss's snappy orders that make you gnash you teeth, but the guy who pushes you out of the way in the dining room.

Hostility will follow wherever you go, because its root is not in the other person but in your own heart. And no matter how fast you run or how far you go, you can't get away from yourself.

Grin-and-Bear-It Kit

Next we consider the *Ignore-It-and-Maybe-It-Will-Go-Away Kit*, which is closely related to the *Grin-and-Bear-It Kit*. Both approaches refuse to deal with distressing situations, one by refusing to admit they exist and the other by refusing to admit you are bothered by them. Both lead to the unhealthy suppression of negative emotions, which inevitably ends in an explosion of the destructive hostility you were trying to avoid.

Most of us, at one time or another, put up a good front in an effort to conceal our real feelings. But the person who thinks that doing so will cause the problem to vanish is only deceiving himself and delaying what must eventually be a confrontation with reality. By that time, pent-up emotions may have wreaked havoc with the person's health or brought about other devastating results. The ostrich-like stance of an ignore-it-and-maybe-it-will-go-away attitude is futile. It has been suggested that while "Smile, Though Your Heart Is Breaking" may be a beautiful old song, following that advice may lead to a heart attack!

The Tranquilizer Kit

Perhaps the *Tranquilizer Kit* is the most dangerous and deceptive of all the "do-it-yourself" kits. The increasing use of drugs to control violent or socially unacceptable behavior is frightening. Robert L. Sprague, director of the Institute for Child Behavior and Development at the University of Illinois, estimates that up to six hundred thousand children in the

United States (mostly boys from kindergarten through eighth grade) are presently receiving medication for the out-of-control, compulsively overactive behavior referred to as hyperactivity, or "hyperkinesis." Others estimate that more than twenty percent of all school children are receiving medication such as Ritalin (generic name: methylpheniclate) to render them more receptive to classroom disciplines and teaching. For many children, the use of these drugs is a prerequisite to attending public school.[4]

People being treated for deep depression and hostility may be injected with psychoactive drugs that supposedly help them cope with life more calmly and successfully. But their actual effect is to numb the patient emotionally and to detach him from reality.

Drugs have become an accepted part of life for us all. Lulled into a false security by their ready availability and widespread use, most of us don't stop to think that we are filling our bodies with an addictive, mind-altering drug before we pop that innocent little capsule into our mouths. Yet on January 26, 1975, the Baltimore *Sunday Sun* ran this headline: "Valium Sends More Addicts to Hospital Than Heroin."

Valium is the most frequently prescribed drug for anxiety. People who take it believe it will reduce their fears and hostility, when in fact it may trigger an eruption of rage and violence.

A tranquilizer's only effect is to reduce the patient's perception of his anxiety and hostility; but since these emotions remain in the brain in full force, they continue to exert their harmful effects.

The worst danger comes about when the drug actually "works." Relieved of the perception of anxiety, the patient is only more encouraged to continue avoiding his underlying problems. Since the drug soon wears off, the perception of the anxiety returns and another dose, often stronger, of the drug is taken—just as in the case of alcohol.[5]

So instead of finding release from the bondage of hostility, we acquire another bondage to a drug with no power to effect a cure.

False Religion Kits

Basically, man has always known that hatred and hostility are spiritual issues. When all else fails, he inevitably turns to religion. Sadly, many religions have nothing to do with God or the restorative power of His Word, and the answers they give are as powerless to cure the sickness of the soul as they are to save it from hell.

Most current deceptions stem from false Eastern religions and philosophies. Transcendental meditation, yoga, E.S.T.—all promise inner peace through different forms of chanting, exercise, and relaxation. But medical experts will tell you that while these exercises may give temporary relief, they do nothing to alleviate the problem.

The Word of God is very specific in telling us we are not to participate in practices that have their origins in the worship of pagan gods. No matter how harmless or contemporary they appear, these are still demonically inspired deceptions to keep us from looking to the real source of healing and redemption, the God who created us and whom we can come to know as we read of Him in the Bible. Romans 14:17 says, "For the kingdom of God is not meat and drink; but righteousness, and peace, and joy in the Holy Ghost."

When we enter into a relationship with Jesus Christ, we no longer need "do-it-yourself" kits. He's already done it all for us. Our responsibility is to accept the righteousness, peace of mind, and joy that are our birthrights.

The world has no answer for hostility because hostility's author and greatest promoter is the "prince of this world." The only true solution is to be found in the words of Jesus, the Prince of Peace.

Chapter 7

WHAT JESUS SAID AND DID ABOUT HOSTILITY

Then came Peter to him, and said, Lord, how oft shall my brother sin against me, and I forgive him? till seven times? Jesus saith unto him, I say not unto thee, Until seven times: but, Until seventy times seven (Matt. 18:21,22).

This Scripture passage expresses the Master's heart about hostility. Forgive, not seven times but seventy times seven. There is to be no limit to our forgiveness. Jesus knew that forgiveness destroys hostility. Where there is a willingness to forgive, there is no place for anger, hurt feelings, or bitterness and resentment to take root.

Jesus' Instructions

In the Sermon on the Mount, Jesus gave very specific instructions about how to avoid hostility. "But

I say unto you, That ye resist not evil: but whosoever shall smite thee on thy right cheek, turn to him the other also'' (Matt. 5:39).

This Scripture verse deals with our willingness to remain vulnerable and open. The physical action of being struck in the face can be symbolic of any hurt or wrong we experience at the hands of another. Jesus was not concerned with the injustice of the act, but with the attitude and response of the one who has been wronged.

Through faith and the power of the Holy Spirit, who enables us to do any and all good things, we can learn not to spontaneously *react* in anger, but to retain control of the situation by *choosing* to forgive. It will be possible to "turn the other cheek" instead of hitting back. By this *action* we turn a negative situation into an expression of love and forgiveness, which probably will disarm the other person and very possibly open the door for real reconciliation. At the very least we will be strengthened in our own resolve not to be manipulated by someone else's anger and sin.

Jesus went on to say, "And if any man will sue thee at the law, and take away thy coat, let him have thy cloak also" (Matt. 5:40).

Again Jesus was addressing the attitude of the one being wronged. Life can be unfair. The innocent aren't always vindicated. The best man doesn't always win. Maybe you have worked hard at a job for ten years and your boss promotes someone else who's only been there five years. Or, as in the example Jesus used, perhaps you were taken to court and lost a case you should have won. What is your response going to be? Bitterness? Anger? Resentment? If you allow these things to fester inside, you will lose more than your coat. You will forfeit peace of mind, the joy of life, and the confidence of a right standing before God. That kind of hostility is costly and fruitless.

Instead, Jesus said, give up your rights and privileges. Refuse to fantasize about what might have been or argue about what should have been. Ask the Holy Spirit to help you keep things in the right perspective. The loss of a coat isn't all that tragic. In fact, the loss of a coat *and* a cloak isn't going to destroy your life. But bitterness and resentment will. Jesus was saying that a key to defeating hostility is to recognize what our true treasures and privileges really are.

"And whosoever shall compel thee to go a mile, go with him twain" (Matt. 5:41). I've heard it said that a Roman citizen had the authority to compel any slave to carry his things as far as a mile. This may have been what Jesus was referring to. When someone begins throwing his weight around and making unreasonable demands, it is human nature to dig our heels in and resist. No one likes to be taken advantage of or used for another's selfish purposes. Although for the most part we are no longer legally bound to "walk that mile" with another person, we are constantly facing the demands of family, friends, and employers. The question is, how much are we willing to give joyfully, and how many of those demands are we going to meet with the right attitude?

Jesus said if a man compels you to go a mile, surprise him and go two. By this means you take control of the situation. You are no longer being taken advantage of; rather, you are accepting an opportunity to give, and you will be blessed for it. Since you are doing something of your own free will, resentment has no room to grow.

In all three examples, Jesus was dealing with the heart attitude of the one wronged. In every case, that person would have had "just cause" to be angry, bitter, or resentful.

Obviously, He knew it would not be easy for us to give and forgive as He directed. Nowhere did He suggest we are going to be supernaturally lifted above our natural, human reactions to these difficult situations. But we know that God does not require anything from us that He also doesn't enable us to perform. Clearly, the message is that no matter how extreme or unjust the situation may be, we sons and daughters of God are not to become hostile.

Corrie ten Boom is a living example of one who determined to forgive and who refused to be hostile. In her book *Tramp for the Lord* Corrie recounts a particularly poignant and difficult confrontation she had with her own struggle to forgive. In a church in Munich she met one of the men who had been a guard at Ravensbruck, the Nazi concentration camp in which she was imprisoned and where her sister Betsie died.

It was 1947, and she had come from Holland to defeated Germany with the message that God forgives. As the man thrust out his hand to her he said, "A fine message, Fraulein! How good it is to know that, as you say, all our sins are at the bottom of the sea!"

Corrie, who moments before had spoken so glibly of forgiveness, now found herself fumbling in her pocketbook rather than taking the man's hand. She remembered only too well the leather crop swinging from his belt and the cruelties the prisoners had endured.

The man explained that he had been a guard at Ravensbruck, but that since that time he had become a Christian. He knew God had forgiven him for the cruel things he had done there, he said, but he wanted to know if Corrie, too, would forgive him. Again he reached out his hand.

Seconds seemed like hours as Corrie wrestled inwardly. Could the memory of Betsie's slow, terrible death be cleared away with a handshake? Yet Corrie knew God had forgiven her own sins again and again—could she do any less for someone who had wronged her and now sought her forgiveness?

She prayed that Jesus would help her.

Numbly she raised her hand to his, and as they grasped she felt a healing warmth through her whole being. "I forgive you, brother, with all my heart!" she cried.

But even as she spoke she knew it was not her love; she had been powerless to love on her own. She could only love by the power of the Holy Spirit.

Jesus gave us a classic and beautiful example of forgiveness in the story of the prodigal son. An ungrateful son rebelled against his parents, demanded his inheritance, and left home, only to lose everything and come back repentant and willing to be a servant in his father's house. Instead, his father welcomed him home with open arms and ordered a great feast to celebrate his return.

But his brother was angry and resentful and refused

to enter into the festivities. When his father asked why, he replied, "Because I've been the good son, doing everything you wanted, and you've never given me a party like this."

The brother was jealous and filled with pious indignation over what he regarded as unfair treatment. His hurt pride made it impossible for him to enter into the family's joy or to empathize with his brother's situation. It seems that in his eyes his brother's greatest sin was repenting and coming home again.

This brother's hostility should be a reminder to all of us to guard against any judgmental spirit that might keep us from wholeheartedly welcoming back into our church or circle of acquaintances those who wander away, fall into sin, and then return broken and needing our love and understanding to become whole again.

The Spiritual Consequences of Hostility

In Matthew 5:21,22 Jesus dealt with the spiritual consequences of hostility.

Ye have heard that it was said by them of old time, Thou shalt not kill; and whosoever shall kill shall be in danger of the judgment: But I say unto you, That whosoever is angry with his brother without a cause shall be in danger of the judgment: and whosoever shall say to his brother, Raca, shall be in danger of the council: but whosoever shall say, Thou fool, shall be in danger of hell fire.

Most of us have no conception of the spiritual dynamic of feelings such as anger and hate when directed toward another person. When released in a healthy way, that dynamic can be positive, breathing new life into relationships and personalities. But when allowed to ferment into hostility, it can be deathly, slowly squeezing the life out of vital areas of the soul.

At the same time, Jesus warned that harboring hostile feelings places us in danger of "judgment" and "hell fire."

An Example to Follow

By far, the most profound commentary we have on hostility is not what Jesus said about it, but how He dealt with it personally. From the moment He was born, Jesus was confronted with others' hatred, fear, and resentment. Barely hours old, He was forced to flee the mass slaughter of newborns that King Herod had ordered in hopes of catching Jesus among them.

Jesus' early years were quiet enough. "And Jesus increased in wisdom and stature, and in favor with God and man" (Luke 2:52). As long as He conformed to the accepted way of thinking and living, He was liked and encouraged. But the moment He stepped outside that familiar pattern and began proclaiming His message and manifesting His authority, His existence became a threat, challenging the traditional foundations of man's relationship to God and man's relationship to man. Those who could not accept the truth and the transformation of thought and life it demanded became hostile and fearful, desiring only to silence His voice.

Matthew 8 tells about a demon-possessed man who lived among some tombs in the country of the Gergesenes. The man was violent and would attack anyone who passed that way. Jesus freed that man from his torment by casting the devils into a herd of pigs, which promptly ran down a steep hill into the sea and drowned.

> And they that kept them fled, and went their ways into the city, and told every thing, and what was befallen to the possessed of the devils. And, behold, the whole city came out to meet Jesus: and when they saw him, they besought him that he would depart out of their coasts. And he entered into a ship, and passed over, and came into his own city (Matt. 8:33–9:1).

The people didn't understand what had happened. They were angry at the loss of the pigs and frightened by the inexplicable events. Their anger and fear produced hostility that closed their minds and their eyes to a miracle. No one was the least bit concerned about the man who had been delivered. Somehow his miraculous transformation was overshadowed by the loss of the pigs.

Yet Jesus didn't argue the point with the people. He didn't stand the delivered man up in front of them and say, "Look what I did!" He didn't call them a bunch of selfish ingrates and swear never to come back again. He simply got in a boat and left quietly. When we don't want Jesus around, He doesn't get angry. He just goes away. But He never harbors a grudge.

Jesus came back to these people at a later date. In the

meantime, the people had calmed down and become conscious of the man who had been freed from the devils. He had told everyone what God had done for him, and when Jesus returned the people were ready to listen.

Jesus knew how to be patient with people's fears and insecurities. Since He knew their hearts, He was tolerant of those who were motivated by an honest desire to know God, even if occasionally they were a little hard of hearing or stubborn. But when they were motivated by greed or selfish ambition, He was capable of the righteous anger and indignation He demonstrated against the money changers in the temple. This incident in Jesus' life substantiates the premise that anger in itself is not always a sin nor a negative force. While there is no room in our lives for bitter hostility, at times anger is appropriate.

Certainly anger is a difficult emotion to control. Not only does it arouse our adrenaline and cause a whole series of physical changes within our bodies, but it can sometimes cause us to do or say things that under ordinary circumstances we might not do.

Perhaps such was the case with Jesus that day when He released His anger with "a scourge of small cords," driving the money changers out of the temple and scattering sheep, oxen, doves, and people in the process (see John 2:13–17). The important teaching here, however, is that Jesus got angry and showed it in a demonstration that left no uncertainty in people's minds. This kind of anger is often called "righteous anger."

In this instance, and in other situations where we catch a glimpse of an angry Jesus, we are given an insight into the heart of the Man sent from God. There are those who mistakenly picture Jesus as being "meek and mild." One writer tells of overhearing a woman in a Bible study class say, "I am tired of a little, old, skinny, emaciated Jesus." He was anything but either of these portrayals.

There are those who struggle with the idea of Jesus' being angry. "Isn't this a contradiction of what the Bible says?" they ask. They find it difficult to reconcile one verse in the Bible that tells us not to be angry with other verses that portray an angry God and an angry Jesus.

Each incident in which we see God or Jesus angry must be considered within its context. There is appropriate anger, and there is questionable or inappropriate anger. Malicious, vindictive rage is always inappropriate; we never see God or His Son responding in that way.

A careful study of the various words for "anger" in their original languages sheds light upon this matter. Generally, when the Bible speaks of God's anger, it refers to justified anger and righteous indignation. Many such examples can be found in the Old Testament especially. (See, for instance, Num. 11:1.) Similar references can be found in the New Testament in such places as Hebrews 3:11, Romans 9:22, and Mark 3:5.

For the Christian who wishes to use anger aright, the question uppermost in his thinking must always be: Will this dishonor the Lord and weaken my Christian stance? If so, it would be inappropriate anger. And even if it is right to be angry about something, how I express that anger will largely determine whether I bring dishonor or glory to God.

The Bible gives us guidelines for handling our anger properly. Our feelings and emotions were given to us by the Lord, so in and of themselves they are not sinful. But it is the manner in which they are used that determines the rightness or wrongness of a given emotion.

A good guideline for the Christian to remember is James 1:19. "Let every man be swift to hear, slow to speak, slow to wrath." (Similar verses can be found in Eccl. 7:9, Prov. 15:18, Titus 1:7, Ps. 103:8; 145:8, and Neh. 9:17.)

When you are tempted to show your anger in an inappropriate way, think of Psalm 37:8: "Cease from anger, and forsake wrath: fret not thyself in any wise to do evil."

I read recently of a woman who buys chipped china at garage sales for pennies. When her anger and frustration build, she goes into her garage and throws the old cups and plates at the walls. By the time she has vented her anger, she ends up laughing. Doing something physical when we are upset or angry will often clear our bloodstreams of the stimulant the fury produced.

In the case of Jesus showing His anger in the temple, there is general agreement among Bible scholars and others that for Him *not* to have responded to that situation would have been displeasing to the Father. We must recognize that in our own lives, as in Jesus' life, there are times when we may be sinning by *not* getting angry.

Along these lines, Dr. Jack Hayford made this observation:

To see both sides of Jesus . . . is to see the need for compassion, for care, for concern, for weeping with those that weep, for sympathy, for groaning, for aching deeply because of what you sense transpiring in human lives. And it is to learn the place and time for anger, when we see Satan's wiles successfully destroying; for indignation, when the adversary's program violates territory that is rightfully Christ's; for boldness, when demonic hordes announce their presence; for attack, when the Holy Spirit prompts an advance which faith can make but before which our flesh quails.[1]

Jesus has appropriately been described as "the Man of Sorrows." Scorned and rejected by His own people, hated and feared by the religious leaders of the day, He was lied about and plotted against. In the end He was betrayed by His own disciple, forsaken by His closest friends, and condemned to death by the very ones He had come to save.

Jesus had a "right" to be hostile. Yet He lived His life without hostility. He taught, "Love your enemies, bless them that curse you, do good to them that hate you, and pray for them which despitefully use you, and persecute you" (Matt. 5:44). On the cross in the midst of the greatest possible physical torment, He prayed, "Father, forgive them; for they know not what they do" (Luke 23:34). Jesus died without hostility.

It is possible that the most personally devastating hurt for Jesus was Peter's denial. The ones who called for His crucifixion didn't know Him. They were motivated out of fear, because He challenged their authority and control over the people. For them, His death was politically expedient rather than a personal matter.

But Peter was a different matter. He had been Jesus' companion, disciple, and friend.

Yet on that blessed morning when the women found the empty tomb, the angel said, "But go your way, tell his disciples *and Peter* that he goeth before you into Galilee: there shall ye see him, as he said unto you" (Mark 16:7, italics added).

Jesus knew the emotional anguish Peter was experiencing over what he had done. He could have let him agonize, but instead Jesus singled Peter out in a way that let him know he was forgiven and wanted. "Go tell my disciples and Peter . . . *especially* Peter!"

Jesus returned love for hate, forgiveness for abuse, and life for death. By His Spirit we can and must do the same.

Chapter 8

HOSTILITY AND THE END TIMES

Today's hostility is, I believe, a fulfillment of prophecy. The Scriptures describe the last days preceding Jesus' return as a time of growing hostility, evil, and destruction in the world. We are told that life will be "as the days of Noah" (Matt. 24:37).

Following are some examples of what I believe the Scriptures mean by "as the days of Noah."

Crime

Crime rates will soar to an uncontrollable high. People will live in fear of their lives, suspiciously guarding themselves not only from strangers but also from neighbors and acquaintances they no longer trust.

Divorce

Divorce statistics will skyrocket, their ever-increasing number making a mockery out of the sacred vows meant to last a lifetime. The marriage ceremony will become so meaningless that some people will do away with it altogether, choosing simply to live together.

Sexual Perversion

Sexual perversion will gradually become acceptable under the guise of sexual freedom. Man's thinking will be so tainted and corrupt that he will think it noble to support an individual's right to enter into unnatural relationships. Homosexuality will be widely accepted and even defended as an alternate life-style.

Violence

Violence will be a part of everyday life. Wife-beating and child abuse will be epidemic, as will murder, rape, and other forms of destructive behavior.

Practice of the Occult

The practice of the occult, demon worship, and other false religions will become widespread. As they did in the days of Noah, people will turn from God and look to the stars or to their own understanding for the answers to life.

"Wait a minute," you may be saying. "You are not

describing some futuristic 'Sodom and Gomorrah'—but my home town, here and now!"

That's right. The signs are unmistakable. We are living in those last days Jesus spoke about, and the worst times of unleashed hostility are still ahead. That is why it is imperative that we know without a shadow of a doubt how to handle hostility in our lives.

Progress, with all its technological advancements; science, with its theories and formulas; education, with its vast accumulation of knowledge; civilization, with all its sophisticated laws and governing systems—none of these have been able to rid us of the plague of hostility. In fact, in many ways they appear only to have aggravated the problem by giving man a false sense of his own importance. This deceptive feeling of self-sufficiency causes him to rely more and more upon his own abilities and accomplishments and less and less upon God, until the Almighty finally is pushed out of the picture entirely and man becomes his own god.

The Universal Void

This gross impertinence has left man at the mercy of his own weakness and ineptitude and has created an enormous void in his soul. Man was created to have fellowship with God, and without that relationship he is incomplete and constantly searching.

Augustine's well-known statement bears repeating: "Thou madest us for thyself, and our heart is restless, until it repose in thee." There is a universal need for

God, an incompleteness that only can be met by Him.

People seek to fill this void in all sorts of ways, in order to still the restlessness within their souls.

In many cases, the futility of that search has produced a hostility toward "dead religion," which some men mistakenly equate with a personal relationship with God. In his book *The Whole Person in a Broken World*, Dr. Paul Tournier writes:

> . . . modern man appears to be disgusted with the religion for which he nevertheless feels a homesickness. He has repressed it, banished it from his life, proclaimed the exclusion of everything beyond the reach of the senses. He has consummated a great rift between the spiritual and the temporal world. And ever since, he has lived in a tragic duality.[1]

This general turn away from organized religion is symbolic of a broader hostility toward all institutions. People who were once regarded with great respect and honor now live in fear of being dragged into court for making mistakes or for not living up to someone else's expectations. Recently a pastor was taken to court by bereaved parents because his counseling failed to prevent their son from committing suicide. And this is not an isolated case.

Many doctors charge exorbitant fees, not because the cost of medicine is so high but because their insurance rates reflect the number of malpractice suits they may have to defend themselves against. (Of course, where there is legitimate cause, a doctor should be made to pay for his incompetency. But often a lawsuit is merely an expression of rage that a doctor couldn't perform the impossible or be superhuman in his efforts.)

Even teachers are not exempt from this kind of attack from students and irate parents.

Spiritual and Emotional Apathy

The result of all this legal finger-pointing is that people are afraid to get involved. Doctors stand by helplessly and watch an accident victim's life ebb away, knowing that if they try to help and are successful they'll be heroes, but if they fail they'll probably end up in court accused of being little more than murderers.

Some pastors water down their doctrines and rely solely on psychology books when counseling, afraid that declaring the biblical absolutes of right and wrong might offend the current morality.

A friend of mine visited a large, growing church of some renown. He looked with interest at the smiling, well-dressed people hurrying this way and that, while he listened to his host point out the buildings and describe the various programs the church had to offer.

"Well, it all seems to be working," my friend acknowledged. "Everyone certainly seems to have found what they were looking for."

The host replied smugly, "Oh, yes! This isn't like some other churches I've been to. You can be Buddhist, or Mormon, or Hindu and feel comfortable here!"

This spiritual and emotional apathy has infected us

all, causing us to draw back at the first sign of trouble or controversy. We fear the price of involvement will be more than we want to pay. Even our laws and court systems often seem to penalize the innocent in an attempt to protect the rights of the guilty. We read in the newspapers about people sitting by passively listening to pitiful cries for help just outside their doors. The intensified hostility of these last days has hardened our hearts and gradually drained us of compassion for the suffering of others.

Consumer Hostility

Our world lives under the constant harassment of a contentious spirit that delights in pitting us against one another. On the whole, society is fearful and un-trusting, constantly expecting the worst instead of the best. We see this skepticism clearly evidenced by the new "consumerism" that is sweeping the country.

Healthy as it may be in the long run, this consumer crusade against poor quality and false advertising has given fresh impetus to myriad legal suits in which manufacturers are threatened with fines or punishments for the slightest technical infraction, whether it be because of conflicting government regulations or their own negligence.

Certainly the consumer has a right to be protected and a right to the full and prompt redress of his legitimate grievances. But this right is easily abused and distorted by turning our courts of law into mere collection agencies. As history has taught us, the only ones to profit from this proliferation of lawsuits are lawyers.

Another great problem this country faces is the basic dishonesty our hostility and disrespect for others has created. Insurance companies get cheated out of billions of dollars every year because of fake accidents and false claims. Large companies lose inestimable amounts of money to dishonest employees and executives who think nothing of "padding the expense account a little." Even the most upright citizens find it hard to be totally honest when it comes to filling out their tax forms.

Rebellion Against Authority

All of this is the result of a basic hostility and rebellion against those in authority over us. Since there is no higher authority than God, He has become the object of man's greatest rebellion. There are people who would sue Him if they could!

Not since the days of Noah have men dared to flaunt their hostility and disdain for God so openly. People are no longer brought up to have a healthy respect for God. Where once they questioned quietly in their hearts, they now openly express their contempt and unbelief. The precious name of Jesus is spit out of the mouth of unbelievers in anger more often than it is lovingly spoken by believers in praise and worship.

One of the most common arguments against God today is, "If there is a God, why does He allow all the suffering in the world?" The fact that men blame and curse God instead of looking within themselves and repenting of their evil ways is prophetic. According to the Bible, some people will harden their hearts and refuse to repent right up to the end.

During the time of great Tribulation the armies of the world will be angry with God.

> And the nations were angry, and thy wrath is come, and the time of the dead, that they should be judged, and that thou shouldest give reward unto thy servants the prophets, and to the saints, and them that fear thy name, small and great; and shouldest destroy them which destroy the earth (Rev. 11:18).

At one point God will pour out His wrath upon the earth in the form of great plagues and heat.

> And men were scorched with great heat, and blasphemed the name of God, which hath power over these plagues: and they repented not to give him glory (Rev. 16:9).

People won't think about confessing their sin and getting right with God but will set themselves against Him even more stubbornly and be condemned by their own hostility and unrepentant spirits.

The Disintegration of the Family

When people don't have a healthy relationship with God, their relationships with others soon become perverted. Micah 7:6 predicts what family life will be like just before the Tribulation.

For the son dishonoreth the father, the daughter riseth up against her mother, the daughter-in-law against her mother-in-law; a man's enemies are the men of his own house.

How often I hear parents complain of this very thing. "My children have no respect for what I am and what I stand for. They want to do things their way. They don't listen any more!"

The disintegration of the family is already of great concern to those who understand its dire implications. We live in a world where maternal and paternal instinct are more matters of choice than natural responses. A new life is assigned little or no value; if it is inconvenient it is readily aborted or disowned at birth. It has even been proposed by certain humanists that parents should be given three days after the birth of a baby to decide whether or not they want to keep it. If not, it would be "humanely" disposed of.

Many children grow up feeling like interruptions in their parents' lives, while parents struggle pathetically to gain their children's love and respect without investing the necessary time and discipline. The trend of role reversal between mothers and fathers, the strong effort of some to erase sexual definitions, the increase in divorce, and the introduction of the homosexual "family unit" have steadily eaten away at the foundations of traditional family life.

This erosion of family relationships is resulting in more and more incidents like the one reported on recent newscasts about a twelve-year-old girl who set her parents' bed on fire in the middle of the night. Another young man kept his elderly mother virtually prisoner in her own home, physically and verbally abusing her until neighbors finally reported their suspicions to the police and the young man was arrested.

Hostility within the family unit will grow in intensity until Jesus returns; only those relationships based on the principles of God's Word will be capable of natural expressions of love, respect, and loyalty.

Hostility Between Management and Labor

In the last days management and labor are going to be in deadly contest. We see the first stirrings of this conflict in the massive move toward socialism throughout the world. Even here in the United States, which was founded upon the concepts of free enterprise and democracy, we find a growing socialist tendency influencing our thinking and even creeping into our politics. But neither socialism nor any other form of government can solve the world's problems, because it is impossible to abolish hatred, greed, and hostility from men's hearts through legislation. When men refuse to acknowledge their sin, they look elsewhere for a logical scapegoat.

The Antichrist

Deceptions will increase as the world prepares for the appearance of the Antichrist. Daniel 8:23–25 describes Daniel's vision of the end times.

> And in the latter time of their kingdom, when the transgressors are come to the full, a king of fierce countenance, and understanding dark sentences, shall stand up (v. 23).

This verse refers to the Antichrist. He will be a man who has an answer for everything.

> And his power shall be mighty, but not by his own power: and he shall destroy wonderfully, and shall prosper, and practice, and shall destroy the mighty and the holy people (v. 24).

The Antichrist will have demonic power to support him, and he will desire to destroy the Jewish people.

> And through his policy also he shall cause craft to prosper in his hand; and he shall magnify himself in his heart, and by peace shall destroy many: he shall also stand up against the Prince of princes; but he shall be broken without hand (v. 25).

The Antichrist will bring prosperity to the whole world for a time, and men will say, "Who is like this one? Let us serve him!" (see Rev. 13:4). He will control the United Nations, and he will destroy the entire world. At the appointed time, when wickedness is at its peak, a man will come whose fierceness will be felt by all the inhabitants of the earth.

In the last days the devil will actually walk the earth, with great wrath.

> Therefore rejoice, ye heavens, and ye that dwell in them. Woe to the inhabiters of the earth and of the sea! for the devil is come down unto you, having great

wrath, because he knoweth that he hath but a short time (Rev. 12:12).

At this time hostility will be at its peak. People will be the victims not only of their own hostility but also of Satan's anger. The resultant upheaval will be so great that Matthew 24:22 says, "Except those days should be shortened, there should no flesh be saved: but for the elect's sake those days shall be shortened."

Just at the point when hostility is about to destroy mankind completely, Jesus will return.

And I saw heaven opened, and behold a white horse; and he that sat upon him was called Faithful and True, and in righteousness he doth judge and make war. . . . And he was clothed with a vesture dipped in blood: and his name is called The Word of God. . . . And he hath on his vesture and on his thigh a name written, KING OF KINGS, AND LORD OF LORDS (Rev. 19:11,13,16).

Only Christ, the King of Kings, will destroy hostility and its direct cause—Satan.

In speaking of the last days, Jesus said:

Now learn a parable of the fig tree; When his branch is yet tender, and putteth forth leaves, ye know that summer is nigh: So likewise ye, when ye shall see all these things, know that it is near, even at the doors (Matt. 24:32,33).

Let us open our eyes and our minds to recognize just where we are in the course of history. The Bible says that in the last days there will be a great falling away. But it also says that God will pour out His Spirit upon all flesh. Our heart attitudes will decide whether we will be susceptible to deception or available to that outpouring of the Holy Spirit.

Chapter 9

FACING UP TO HOSTILITY

You've heard it said that recognizing a problem is half the battle. So it is with hostility. Most of us have no difficulty seeing hostility in others but identifying it in our own lives is another matter. It is very easy for us to justify our feelings or to label them as something they are not.

If you detect suppressed hostility in someone and, out of love and concern, you ask them, "Why are you hostile?" more than likely you will get an emphatic denial. Moreover, the person questioned will no doubt react with hostility. Furthermore, they will be quick to try to convince you that they are anything but hostile. "I'm not hostile, but I am hurt," they might say, or "I've been left out and ignored, and I'm really disappointed."

We must stop making excuses and face up to the problem of hostility—not just in other people but within our own hearts and minds—if we are ever to make a significant difference in the world around us. We may not be able to stop the acceleration of hostility throughout the earth, but we can protect our own private world of thoughts and attitudes and personal relationships from its ravaging effects.

Civilized man has proved that he is capable of behaving in a most uncivilized way. Lifting a man's mind out of the Dark Ages has nothing to do with lifting his soul out of spiritual darkness. Hostility is a fact of life on planet Earth; it will exist until Jesus comes. Evil and iniquity will be with us until the prince of this world is cast down. For this reason we must learn to cope with sin and hostility in a godly way.

Pray, Talk, and Then Do Something!

Some might say, "Brother Sumrall, you are writing about a spiritual problem, so let's not talk about it; let's pray about it."

I say, "Let's do both." Prayer is an essential weapon in the battle, and I am by no means disparaging its power and effect. But the Word says that faith without works is dead, and I believe that American Christians have been silent for too long. A recent nationwide poll revealed that fifty-eight percent of all Americans profess to be born again! It is time we spoke up for righteousness with a loud voice. We *can* make a difference.

But people won't hear us if we refuse to be honest about our own failures and weaknesses. We must take the positive steps necessary to live lives that manifest the power and love of God in practical, everyday situations. One of those steps is facing up to and dealing with our own hostility.

One's ability to deal with anger, hatred, prejudice, jealousy, and other hostile emotions depends on his spiritual understanding and his conscious desire to overcome the problems. Only when we recognize them, admit they are our own, and submit them to God's transforming power can we be truly free. Unfortunately, some people have buried their hostility so deep that they are totally unaware that it is there. There are people who make it a practice never to argue, thereby claiming they have learned to control their tempers. The truth is, their hostility is being suppressed. Avoiding arguments and maintaining a calm exterior all the time is not realistic.

We come back to Ephesians 4:26. "Be ye angry, and sin not: let not the sun go down upon your wrath." God does not tell us that in order to be holy we must put on some false, sanctimonious show; rather, He encourages us to express our indignation over things that are wrong. By this means we keep our emotional system cleaned out; the anger has no opportunity to dam up inside and cause problems.

The Dangers of Passive Hostility

It is a fact of life that there is no such thing as a person who never gets angry. There are only those who express their anger, and those who suppress it. According to Alan Loy McGinnis, people who don't express their anger in a healthy way not only develop psychological problems but also put their important personal relationships in jeopardy. The mild-mannered man may appear to be more popular, but according to McGinnis, popularity is not synonymous with intimacy. The man who is superficially liked by everyone is rarely loved deeply by anyone.

McGinnis lists four reasons he believes this is true of the passively hostile person. (1) He is never perceived as open, so he is hard for others to relate to. (2) He is dull. People prefer the company of others with more passion. (3) If he cannot show anger he will be inept at showing love as well. (4) Without knowing it, he poisons his relationships with his passive hostility.[1]

It is a recognized fact that passively hostile people are much harder to get along with than those who erupt with honest, direct anger. Passively hostile people show by their actions that they have been hurt, but they deny that anything is wrong. The result of living this way is that the acids of accumulating grudges eat away at their relationships.

Elizabeth Skoglund, who wrote *To Anger, With Love,* believes anger is unavoidable when two people relate openly and spontaneously, and that it can be a positive force when expressed in a healthy way.

I have heard this inevitable "abrasiveness" in relationships described as a "sandpaper effect." One of the major purposes for God's bringing two people together, whether in marriage or as friends, is so that each may encourage the other. That encouragement can be pleasant or not, depending on how receptive we are to what we are being told. Much of our "remodeling" requires a sanding away of rough surfaces and sharp edges—not particularly comfortable but necessary.

When we recognize this constant rubbing not as an irritant, but as the loving hand of our heavenly Father polishing us to a high shine in which others will see the reflection of Christ, it becomes easier to accept without giving way to hostility.

Overt Hostility

For the overtly hostile person, the first step in facing up to hostility is admitting his attitude is wrong. This presents a challenge. Hostility usually is triggered by someone else's negative or thoughtless action toward us, so it is easy to excuse or rationalize our hostile response.

When our hostility has grounds for defense, we often choose to nurture our feelings, feeding our anger instead of releasing it and trusting the Lord to rectify the situation.

A pair of newlyweds have their first no-holds-barred argument, and it ends with the bride making a dramatic retreat to the bedroom and locking the door. For the next half hour, her distraught young husband listens to her loud sobs. Finally, unable to stand it any longer, he knocks on the door.

"Please, Honey, open the door. I want to apologize."

"Later," she answers. "I'm not through being mad yet!"

Something inside the human heart *enjoys* being angry when we feel we've been wronged. We don't want to let go of it; we savor our indignation and reaffirm our position as a "victim."

Some people become so steeped in what they regard as "justified anger" that it becomes the strongest part of their personalities, tainting every other area of thought and expression. Their anger protects them from feelings of vulnerability and helplessness, and so becomes a strange ally in their battle against despair. Soon, their hostility becomes a motivation rather than a result, a living thing that no longer can be traced to any one hurt, but actually propagates itself.

At this point a person's whole identity can become directly linked to his anger, which becomes very difficult to isolate and identify. When this happens, human logic no longer has any effect. Only the Word of God, which is sharper than any two-edged sword, can cut through to the root and cull it out.

For this reason Psalm 37:7–9 urges:

> Rest in the LORD, and wait patiently for him: fret not thyself because of him who prospereth in his way, because of the man who bringeth wicked devices to pass. Cease from anger, and forsake wrath: fret not thyself in any wise to do evil. For evildoers shall be cut off: but those that wait upon the LORD, they shall inherit the earth.

No matter what injustice we may have suffered or how unkind someone may have been, we are responsible for our own actions and attitudes. We have available to us all the resources necessary to have victory over sinful or negative feelings through Christ our Lord. Once we face up to this responsibility, we are ready to take action to destroy hostility in our lives.

Chapter 10

HOW TO DESTROY HOSTILITY

One cannot improve upon God's method for dealing with hostility. In Galatians 5:16–25 we are given the directions for living a love-inspired, love-mastered, and love-driven life.

Walking in the Spirit

This I say then, Walk in the Spirit, and ye shall not fulfill the lust of the flesh. For the flesh lusteth against the Spirit, and the Spirit against the flesh: and these are contrary the one to the other: so that ye cannot do the things that ye would. But if ye be led of the Spirit, ye are not under the law. Now the works of the flesh are manifest, which are these; Adultery, fornication, uncleanness, lasciviousness, idolatry, witchcraft, hatred, variance, emulations, wrath, strife, seditions, heresies, envyings, murders, drunkenness, revellings, and such like: of the which I tell you before, as I have also told you in time past, that they who do such things shall not inherit the kingdom of God. But the fruit of the Spirit is love, joy, peace, long-suffering, gentleness, goodness, faith, meekness, temperance: against such there is no law. And they that are Christ's have crucified the flesh with the affections and lusts. If we live in the Spirit, let us also walk in the Spirit.

Every one of the "works of the flesh" is related to hostility in some way. It is the fruit of the Spirit that counterbalances their negative effects. But while the works of the flesh spring up like weeds in an unattended garden, the fruit of the Spirit must be carefully cultivated. This can be done only through a personal relationship with Jesus Christ, through reading His Word, and through making a conscious effort to pull out the "weeds" as they creep back into our thoughts and actions.

The Power of Confession

Once we face up to hostility, we need to verbally confess it to the Lord. The power of confession cleanses the soul, keeping us open to God's continuous work of redemption in our lives. As we seek to be more like Jesus, we will find the fruit of the Spirit more evident in us. At the same time, our human nature, which leads to hostility, will be more easily subjugated.

For a good tree bringeth not forth corrupt fruit; neither doth a corrupt tree bring forth good fruit. For every tree is known by his own fruit. For of thorns men do

109

not gather figs, nor of a bramble bush gather they grapes. A good man out of the good treasure of his heart bringeth forth that which is good; and an evil man out of the evil treasure of his heart bringeth forth that which is evil: for of the abundance of the heart his mouth speaketh (Luke 6:43–45).

You Are Being Heard

If you want to know who you really are, just listen to what you say. The mouth speaks what is in the heart. If our hearts are bound with cords of bitterness and grudges, we may say the right words but we will communicate our hostility loud and clear by our tone and inflection. But as we humble ourselves and allow the Holy Spirit to transform our hearts and renew our minds, our attitudes and conversation will be a direct reflection of the love of Jesus working in us and through us.

It is only by the mighty power of God that hostility is defeated and driven from our hearts. But certain principles from God's Word provide us with the major weapons for this battle.

Forgiveness

Forgiveness is perhaps the most powerful and essential of these weapons; without it there can be no release from hostility. Forgiveness is an act of the will. It has nothing to do with the rightness or wrongness of our grievance or whether the other person is repentant or not. We must forgive as we have been forgiven.

Many people pray these familiar words: "And forgive us our debts, as we forgive our debtors" (Matt. 6:12). But I wonder how many of us actually think about what we are asking when we say those words.

Jesus said, "If ye forgive not men their trespasses, neither will your Father forgive your trespasses" (Matt. 6:15).

Clearly, if we do not forgive, we shall not be forgiven.

C. S. Lewis, in his book *Mere Christianity*, discussed two things that can help make forgiveness something we do, not just something we talk about doing. (1) Start with smaller hurts, which are more easily forgiven, and work up to the truly heart-crushing injustices life brings. (2) Come to a clearer understanding of what it means to "love thy neighbor as thyself."

> . . . I have not exactly got a feeling of fondness or affection for myself, and I do not even always enjoy my own society. So apparently "Love your neighbor" does not mean "feel fond of him" or "find him attractive." I ought to have seen that before, because, of course, you cannot feel fond of a person by trying. . . .

> . . . a good many people imagine that forgiving your enemies means making out that they are really not such bad fellows after all, when it is quite plain that they are. Go a step further. In my most clear-sighted moments not only do I not think myself a nice man, but I know that I am a very nasty one. I can look at some of the things I have done with horror and loathing. So apparently I am allowed to loathe and hate some of the things my enemies do. Now that I come to think of it, I remember Christian teachers telling me long ago that I must hate a bad man's actions, but not hate the bad man: or, as they would say, hate the sin but not the sinner.

For a long time I used to think this a silly, straw-splitting distinction: how could you hate what a man did and not hate the man? But years later it occurred to me that there was one man to whom I had been doing this all my life—namely myself. However much I might dislike my own cowardice or conceit or greed, I went on loving myself. There had never been the slightest difficulty about it. In fact, the very reason why I hated the things was that I loved the man. Just because I loved myself, I was sorry to find that I was the sort of man who did those things. Consequently, Christianity does not want us to reduce by one atom the hatred we feel for cruelty and treachery. We ought to hate them. Not one word of what we have said about them needs to be unsaid. But it does want us to hate them in the same way in which we hate things in ourselves: being sorry that the man should have done such things, and hoping, if it is any way possible, that somehow, sometime, somewhere, he can be cured and made human again.[1]

Honest Confrontation

This willingness to forgive others does not obligate us to swallow our feelings when we honestly believe a brother has wronged us. This kind of suppression can lead to the unhealthy emotional buildup that produces the very hostility we are determined to destroy. Matthew 18:15 tells us how to handle these situations.

> Moreover if thy brother shall trespass against thee, go and tell him his fault between thee and him alone: if he shall hear thee, thou hast gained thy brother.

Honest confrontation aimed toward reconciliation will safeguard us from a buildup of negative emotions and help to keep lines of communication open. If we can talk about our feelings honestly, we have a much better chance of keeping them under control and of resolving the issue without damaging the relationship or our own spiritual and emotional health.

Prayer

Prayer is a mighty weapon against hostility. If we truly believe that "whatsoever thou shalt bind on earth shall be bound in heaven: and whatsoever thou shalt loose on earth shall be loosed in heaven" (Matt. 16:19), then we know we are never helpless in any situation. We have all the resources of heaven at our disposal. This knowledge in itself should help check the hostility-producing fears and frustrations that come with a seemingly hopeless situation. Christians are never hopeless or helpless, because they serve a God who can do anything and who answers prayer.

There are times when bondage to hostility is so deep-seated that deliverance is needed. If this is the case, don't be afraid. Talk to your pastor or a discerning Christian counselor. Jesus came to heal the brokenhearted and deliver the captives. The bonds of hostility are strong, and you may need the prayers of other believers to break their hold.

Accept and Appreciate Others

Accepting other people and circumstances is another practical step in destroying hostility. Don't torture yourself with what might have been. Don't allow Satan to needle you into dissatisfaction with your lot in life. Trust God, knowing that He gives each of His children exactly what he or she needs.

Get in the habit of appreciating other people's good qualities. Will Rogers was famous for his saying, "I never met a man I didn't like." He approached others expecting the best, and people usually made an effort not to disappoint him. Much of our attitude toward other people is determined long before we even meet them. A positive acceptance of others does much to dispel hostility.

Resist feelings of competitiveness, which can make you resent another's success. Instead, rejoice in your brother's good fortune and do your best to follow Paul's admonition: "Let nothing be done through strife or vainglory; but in lowliness of mind let each esteem other better than themselves" (Phil. 2:3).

If you make the people around you feel good about themselves, you will reap the benefit of their confidence and positive attitude, and hostility will be far less likely to find a foothold.

When conflicts do arise, take time to put yourself in the other person's position. Sometimes this provides an entirely different picture of the situation. If you cannot acquiesce, perhaps you can at least compromise with good humor and grace.

We can avoid overreacting to negative situations if we realize that disagreements are bound to happen in any relationship. Don't have unrealistic expectations of yourself or of others. Recognize that frustration and anger are emotions we all feel at times; the best relationships allow for such feelings.

Parent-Child Relationships

These principles also apply to parent-child relationships. Children are people, too, and they need to express their negative feelings just as adults do. If little Johnny is punished every time he expresses anger or frustration, he will grow up habitually suppressing his negative emotions. With no understanding of how to release those emotions in a healthy way, he becomes a walking time bomb. Parents must teach children appropriate ways to communicate these feelings, without being overly permissive or encouraging emotional self-indulgence.

In this regard it is helpful for parents to understand that anger and sadness are closely related in childhood. A small child has not as yet developed a working understanding of all the varied shades of negative and positive emotions. Instead he lumps them together under far more basic headings such as happy, sad, glad, and mad. Once this is understood it becomes obvious that some expression of anger or frustration is completely normal and to some degree necessary for healthy emotional development.

The following are a few practical suggestions for dealing with the angry or hostile child:

1. Respond to positive efforts and reinforce good behavior. We are quick to tell a child what we don't like. Be equally quick to tell him what we do like.

2. Avoid placing a small child in a situation that you know will provoke or tempt him beyond his emotional ability to control.

3. Teach a child to see humor in even difficult situations. The healthiest people are the ones who have

115

learned to laugh at themselves once in a while.

4. Talk to your child about your feelings regarding his behavior. Don't always just say "no." Explain possible consequences so that the child understands your reasoning. This is what the Bible means by "train up a child in the way he should go" . . . taking the time to instruct as well as to correct.

5. Create clearly defined and easily understood limits.

6. Encourage the child to talk about his feelings and really listen when he does. If a child learns early to verbalize his feelings, he will find it less necessary later to resort to violent or destructive behavior.

7. Show your affection and constantly remind the child that he is loved and wanted.

Teaching a child to deal with his emotions is a most pressing and demanding responsibility for parents because children learn best from examples, not lectures. "Do as I say and not as I do" simply doesn't work. Essential to helping a child handle his anger is the ability on the part of the parent to do the same with his or her feelings of hostility. Angry parents who cannot control their own anger will be unable to help children who have feelings of hostility.

Walter Trobisch tells of observing hostility directed toward children in his travels from country to country. I, too, have observed this. He believes we in the "so-called Christian West" are more guilty of this than parents in Third World countries and some of the Iron Curtain countries.

Trobisch relates this to the abortion problem in this country.

116

It seems to me that there is a direct relationship between the lack of self-acceptance, the hostility toward the body and the hostility toward children. Bringing forth children is a part of the physical dimension of life. He who does not have a positive relationship to his body will find it difficult to reach a positive relationship to the child, who is a fruit of his body.

I wonder whether one of the deepest roots of the abortion problem does not lie here. Could it be that this also is the result of non-self-acceptance which expresses itself in a hostile act against the newborn fruit of the body? Can an expectant mother who wishes to abort her child really love herself? Otherwise how could she act so egotistically?[2]

Hostility is much easier to avoid if we discipline ourselves to deal with the issues as they arise. Don't let a dozen small irritations that could easily be talked out one at a time create a wall of cumulative bad feelings between you and someone else. And be sure your anger is focused upon the real issue, not on someone or something else. For many of us this will take thought and discipline, because it is easy to fall into the habit of using those we feel secure with as emotional "whipping boys."

Parents especially must be careful not to abuse their children by taking advantage of minor offenses to blow off steam, just as anyone in a position of authority must guard himself from abusing his power. It is sad but quite generally true that authority figures tend to be quick to anger. When such individuals can't find an appropriate outlet, they often vent their anger towards someone who can't easily fight back—an employee, a child, a spouse, or an animal.

David Augsburger suggests that another practical way to control hostility is to zero in on the specific behavior we don't like rather than attacking the whole person.

> Next time, try focusing your anger on the person's behavior. Express appreciation for the other as a person, even as you explain your anger at his or her way of behaving. It lets you stay in touch while getting at what you are angry about. And, as Jesus demonstrated, you can be both angry (at behaviors) and loving (toward persons) at the same time.[3]

Refuse to play the "blame game." Since we are all ultimately responsible before God for our own behavior and attitudes, it is a waste of time and energy to attempt to place blame or inflict guilt upon others.

> Blame is powerless to effect change and growth. Blame is powerless to evoke inner-direction and new course correction. . . . Nothing settles old scores like the recognition that everything finally comes out even. That's how it is in any ongoing relationship. If there is blame to be fixed, it includes both persons involved.[4]

Think Before You Speak

Learn to express your feelings clearly. Heated arguments are generally ineffective because it is impossible to think rationally, to speak thoughtfully, and to really hear what the other person is saying when you are in the throes of emotional combat. Instead, take a few moments to think through what you want to say. Count to ten.

By controlling our tongues and reining in our unbridled emotions, we can actually turn negative confrontations into creative and positive exchanges that have the power to break through emotional and communication barriers and establish contact.

Once channels of communication are open, hostility usually gives way to a mutual desire to understand and solve the problem. When this happens, the relationship is strengthened, not weakened. Most of us know how it feels to air grievances and then get the relationship back on the right track.

Anger's Energy: A Positive Force

We needn't always look at anger as an enemy. There are certain things we should be angry about. There are times when God uses anger over evil or injustice in the world to spur men into action against it. Powerful indignation has fired the careers of many influential men. Martin Luther once said, "When I am angry I can write, pray and preach well, for my whole temperament is quickened, my understanding sharpened, and all mundane vexations and temptations depart."

Anger quickens the senses, shooting adrenaline through our bodies and glycogen to our fatigued muscles. It moves the lethargic to action, giving courage for tasks we would never attempt in milder moods.

Anger need not rule our lives; rather, we can rule over it, using it as a positive instrument to produce

119

change and growth. The energy anger produces can be a powerful force when controlled by love and an awareness of the other person's rights and worth.

In *The Friendship Factor,* Alan Loy McGinnis suggests five ways to get angry without being destructive.

1. *"Talk about Your Feelings, Not Your Friend's Faults. . . .* To express our irritation in terms of our feelings, for which we are willing to take responsibility, does not insure protection from our friend's anger, but it is a lot less likely to wave a red flag."[5]

2. *"Stick to One Topic. . . .* The resolution of one problem at a time is difficult enough without pulling in old grievances. The problems should be dealt with as they arise, so that we do not carry around unprocessed anger."[6]

3. *"Allow Your Friend to Respond. . . .* People who walk out during an argument are dirty fighters. If you are angry with your friend, you have a right to express it, but you also have the responsibility to stay and hear the other side. Then there's an opportunity for resolution or compromise."[7]

4. *"Aim for Ventilation, Not Conquest. . . .* The point of showing our loved ones our anger is to ventilate our feelings, not to force them to surrender. Far too many couples suppose that every time there is an argument, one or the other has to apologize. Apologies are sometimes in order and sometimes they are not. Lots of times it clears the air if the two ventilate their emotions, get their hostility out, and then go back to loving each other. No one has to win."[8]

5. *"Balance Criticism with Lots of Affection. . . .* You can get away with many expressions of anger if you balance them with lots of expressions of love."[9]

That last point is very important. Rarely do we forget to tell someone when we are angered, hurt, or irritated by something they have said or done. But frequently we don't think to speak aloud our admiration or appreciation for family members, close friends, or fellow workers. We take the good things for granted, while never missing a chance to point out the bad. People try harder to please when their efforts are acknowledged, and they receive criticism and correction more easily from someone who has already demonstrated his respect and appreciation for them as individuals.

"Walking Love"

Unquestionably, our lives will be stronger, richer, and have more meaning in direct proportion to our willingness to express love. We are to be "walking love" to each other.

Love! Love is the key: God's love for us, our love for ourselves, and our love for others. Hostility may be contagious, but so is love. And where love abounds, hostility cannot thrive. In his book *A Second Touch,* Keith Miller talks about how his revitalized awareness of God's love and concern for him personally helped him to begin seeing and responding to others in a whole new way.

Being conscious of Christ's attention not only affected what I did and said, but what I saw. And just seeing people differently changed entire relationships. There was one man, whom I disliked intensely, whose office was close to ours. He was arrogant and a smart aleck;

he needled people viciously, many of whom, like the secretaries, could only choke back tears of embarrassment and anger. This man was mad at the world. As an angry smart aleck (which is what I saw when I looked at him), he had no use for Christ's love. But as I began to look at this man, being aware that Christ and I were looking at him together, I began to see in the same person a man who was deeply hurt, threatened, and *very* lonely. This is what this man really was inside. It dawned on me that for a man like that, Christ's love could have meaning. When I responded naturally to what I now saw as I looked at this man, he began to drop the facade of anger, and hurt began to come out. Suddenly we were at ease with each other without anything having been said to break down the real person behind his mask, and somehow he knew and felt loved. I was seeing why the saints had come up with such seemingly simple, basic ways to relate. It was not because they were brilliant. Most of them were not. They had a different perspective; and from that spiritual vantage point, they looked at the unsolvable problems other men saw. However, they saw—in the same situations—different problems. They saw problems which could be dealt with through the love and acceptance of God. They saw men as Christ saw them.[10]

Once we begin to see other people as Jesus sees them, with all their hurts, insecurities, and loneliness, we find it possible to love our neighbors and our enemies. We can love those who don't love us or even like us. When they make a little circle and leave us out, we can make a bigger circle and take them in. And there isn't anything they can do about it; they are loved.

Love frees us to allow other people to be what God intended them to be, not what we think they should be. And it helps us to accept our own flaws and frailties. The God who created us accepts our humanity, including our hostile feelings. What He wants is our willingness to yield to His Holy Spirit, so He can turn all our emotions in the right direction.

God can use our anger in positive ways, but it is not enough to give Him only our anger. We must give Him our hearts, our thoughts, our ambitions for the future, and our hurts of the past. We must relinquish our rights to bitterness and resentment, just as Jesus did even as they drove the nails into His hands and feet. We must seek to be filled with an understanding of His will.

> That ye might walk worthy of the Lord unto all pleasing, being fruitful in every good work, and increasing in the knowledge of God; Strengthened with all might, according to his glorious power, unto all patience and longsuffering with joyfulness; Giving thanks unto the Father, which hath made us meet to be partakers of the inheritance of the saints in light: Who hath delivered us from the power of darkness, and hath translated us into the kingdom of his dear Son: In whom we have redemption through his blood, even the forgiveness of sins (Col. 1:10–14).

Jesus' death and resurrection provide a way for us to be free from hostility and from all other sinful bondage. We who are His children are no longer bound to the "works of the flesh." We can resign ourselves to lives of slavery, to old thought patterns and emotional responses, or we can assume the responsibilities of our liberty in Christ Jesus, with all its privileges and demands.

Hostility

The bondage of hostility or the freedom of love, the choice is ours.

"If the Son therefore shall make you free, ye shall be free indeed" (John 8:36).

NOTES

Chapter 1

1. David Augsburger, *Caring Enough To Confront* (Glendale, Calif.: Regal, 1973), p. 11.

Chapter 2

1. Konrad Lorenz, *On Aggression,* trans. Marjorie K. Wilson (New York: Bantam, 1970), n.p.
2. Keith Miller, *A Second Touch* (Waco, Tex.: Word, 1967), p. 156.
3. John Perkins, *Let Justice Roll Down* (Glendale, Calif.: Regal, 1976), p. 163.
4. Ibid., pp. 163, 165.
5. Dr. Jack Hayford, *Prayer Is Invading the Impossible* (Plainfield, N.J.: Logos, 1977), p. 103.
6. Elizabeth R. Skoglund, *To Anger, With Love* (New York: Harper and Row, 1977), p. 21.
7. Ibid., pp. 19, 21.

Hostility

Chapter 3

1. Helen Hosier, *Suicide, A Cry For Help* (Irvine, Calif.: Harvest House, 1978), p. 89.
2. Ibid., p. 91.
3. Alan Loy McGinnis, *The Friendship Factor* (Minneapolis, Minn.: Augsburg, 1979), p. 130.
4. Kenneth L. Fish, *Conflict and Dissent in the High School* (New York: Bruce Publishing Company, 1970), p. 1.
5. Dr. Milton Layden, *Escaping the Hostility Trap* (Englewood Cliffs, N.J.: Prentice-Hall, 1977), p. 136.

Chapter 4

1. Theodora Wells, *Keeping Your Cool Under Fire* (New York: McGraw-Hill, 1980), p. 3.
2. Helen Hosier, *It Feels Good to Forgive* (Irvine, Calif.: Harvest House, 1979), p. 107.

Chapter 5

1. Helen Hosier, *It Feels Good to Forgive* (Irvine, Calif.: Harvest House, 1979) p. 61.
2. Hazel McAlister, *The Hidden Riches of Secret Places* (Nashville, Tenn.: Thomas Nelson, 1980), p. 28.
3. Ibid., pp. 29–30.

Chapter 6

1. Dr. Milton Layden, *Escaping the Hostility Trap* (Englewood Cliffs, N.J.: Prentice-Hall, 1977), p. 26.
2. Ibid.
3. Ibid., p. 18.
4. Joseph N. Bell, "Ritalin and Children: Miracle Drug or Menace?" *Family Weekly*, Nov. 2, 1980.
5. Layden, *Escaping . . .* , pp. 25–26.

Chapter 7

1. Dr. Jack Hayford, *Prayer Is Invading the Impossible* (Plainfield, N.J.: Logos, 1977), p. 45.

Chapter 8

1. Dr. Paul Tournier, *The Whole Person in a Broken World* (New York: Harper and Row, 1964), n.p.

Chapter 9

1. Alan Loy McGinnis, *The Friendship Factor* (Minneapolis, Minn.: Augsburg, 1979), p. 128.

Chapter 10

1. C. S. Lewis, *Mere Christianity* (New York: Macmillan, 1943), pp. 105–106.
2. Walter Trobisch, *Love Yourself* (Downers Grove, Ill.: InterVarsity, 1976), pp. 32–33.
3. David Augsburger, *Caring Enough to Confront* (Glendale, Calif.: Regal, 1973), p. 41.
4. Ibid., pp. 76–77.
5. Alan Loy McGinnis, *The Friendship Factor* (Minneapolis, Minn.: Augsburg, 1979), p. 140.
6. Ibid., p. 142.
7. Ibid.
8. Ibid., p. 143.
9. Ibid., p. 144.
10. Keith Miller, *A Second Touch* (Waco Tex.: Word, 1967), pp. 28–29.